CLASSICS OF IRISH HISTORY
General Editor: Tom Garvin

Original publication dates of reprinted titles are given in brackets

P. S. O'Hegarty, *The Victory of Sinn Féin* (1924)

Walter McDonald, *Some Ethical Questions of Peace and War* (1919)

Joseph Johnston, *Civil War in Ulster* (1913)

James Mullin, *The Story of a Toiler's Life* (1921)

Robert Brennan, *Ireland Standing Firm*
and *Eamon de Valera* (1958)

Mossie Harnett, *Victory and Woe:
The West Limerick Brigade in the War of Independence*

Padraig de Burca and John F. Boyle, *Free State or Republic?
Pen Pictures of the Historic Treaty Session of Dáil Éireann* (1922)

Arthur Clery, *The Idea of a Nation* (1907)

Standish James O'Grady, *To the Leaders of Our Working People*

Michael Davitt, *Jottings in Solitary*

Oliver MacDonagh, *Ireland: The Union and its Aftermath* (1977)

Thomas Fennell, *The Royal Irish Constabulary:
A History and Personal Memoir*

Arthur Griffith, *The Resurrection of Hungary* (1918)

William McComb, *The Repealer Repulsed* (1841)

George Moore, *Parnell and His Island* (1887)

Standish James O'Grady, *Sun and Wind*

IRISH
RECOLLECTIONS

Charlotte Elizabeth Tonna

edited by
Patrick Maume

University College Dublin Press
Preas Choláiste Ollscoile Bhaile Átha Cliath

First published in 1841 as *Personal Recollections*
by Seeley, Jackson & Halliday, London
This abridged version of the 1847 edition first
published by University College Dublin Press, 2004

Introduction © Patrick Maume 2004

ISBN 1-904558-10-0
ISSN 1383-6883

University College Dublin Press
Newman House, 86 St Stephen's Green
Dublin 2, Ireland
www.ucdpress.ie

Cataloguing in Publication data
available from the British Library

Typeset in Ireland in Baskerville by Elaine Shiels, Bantry, Co. Cork
Printed on acid-free paper in Ireland by ColourBooks, Dublin

CONTENTS

INTRODUCTION.

Patrick Maume

Charlotte Elizabeth Tonna,[1] *Biographical Note*

Charlotte Elizabeth Browne was born on 1 October 1790 in
Norwich, daughter of Canon Michael Browne. She had one
brother, John Murray Browne. Their relationship was very
close; Tonna remarks that home education preserved him
from the cynical contempt for women inculcated in boarding
schools. Her father was a firm Tory and opponent of Catholic
Emancipation. Charlotte recalled him speaking of Irish rebel-
lions: "if the events of ninety-eight were not alone sufficient to
deter the English government from [Catholic Emancipation],
nothing could overcome their infatuation". She was shown
where Wycliffite martyrs died in the fifteenth century and
Protestants were burned in the Marian persecutions; she
regarded Mary Tudor as a female Antichrist prefiguring the
final three-and-a-half-year tribulation of the Saints. Aged six,
she encountered an illustrated folio Foxe's Book of Martyrs
(with a paternal admonition that if Papists regained power she
might be martyred). Tonna was deeply influenced by Foxe's
portrayals of Catholicism as heir to ancient paganism, the
Church of England springing from a succession of persecuted
true believers, and England as a second Israel whom God
would defend against continental autocrats while they remained
faithful. (In 1837 she published an abridged Foxe.)

Her parents rewarded good behaviour with Bible readings;
this produced an abiding love for the Bible (encouraging her

later belief that Irish Catholics could be spontaneously converted by hearing it read aloud). At the age of six she developed temporary blindness through excessive reading. She was treated with mercury, to which she attributed her permanent deafness from the age of ten. Her father exchanged his urban parish for the rural living of Bawburgh, believing this would assist her recovery. She was allowed to roam freely, preserved from corsets and foot-binding; her later hostility to the factory system and nostalgia for rural paternalism reflected idealised memories of Bawburgh.

The traditional "chosen people" mentality revived during the Napoleonic Wars; Charlotte regarded Napoleon as a scourge sent by God to punish Popish nations.[2] There were closer threats: "Antichrist bestrode our city, firmly planting there his two cloven hooves of Popery and Socinianism [a form of Unitarianism] . . . elements both of a French revolution and an Irish rebellion". Her father once led a "church and king" mob against radical activists. During the Revolutionary and Napoleonic Wars, George III was portrayed as symbol of national resistance and ideal Christian monarch. Tonna later called him a second Hezekiah – the just king in the last days of the Davidic kingdom, who by implementing God's Law delayed divinely decreed punishment for his predecessors' apostasies. She thought God inspired the king to prevent Catholic Emancipation in 1800, delaying national apostasy until the Evangelical Revival took root; she interpreted his madness as divine mercy withdrawing him from a degenerate world, and suggested the angels with whom he conversed were not imaginary. When fellow-ultras criticised George IV and William IV, she urged respect for "the progeny of our Hezekiah".[3]

Tonna's illnesses and early infatuation with Shakespeare stimulated her imagination to an extent she later thought satanic. "Reality became insipid, almost hateful to me . . . I imbibed a thorough contempt for women, children, and household affairs". As a teenager she composed witty political squibs.

The break-up of the Browne household began in 1806 when John went to the Peninsular War; Charlotte, entranced by military glamour, helped to overcome parental objections. In 1808 Canon Browne died of a stroke. The Canon secured his prebend relatively late in life; he had bought an annuity for his wife, but Charlotte was left financially insecure. She considered becoming a professional writer, but was saved from this satanic temptation (as she later thought) by another misfortune.

Her brother showed her letters to fellow-officers; Captain George Phelan decided to marry the writer. Everyone who knew the "headstrong" Charlotte and "excitable" Phelan disagreed,[4] but the couple were obdurate. Soon after their marriage, Captain Phelan was assigned to Nova Scotia. Charlotte alarmed the ship's company by opening a window during an Atlantic storm to admire its sublime terrors; on shore she revelled in galloping a high-spirited horse, later attributing her unbroken neck to divine interposition. The marriage soured quickly. Charlotte lamented the near-absence of servants and her lack of household skills. Scattered references suggest Captain Phelan beat her;[5] her most widely circulated anti-slavery poem is "On the Flogging of Women", and her celebrated poem on the siege of Derry depicts the Maiden City repelling male wooers who combine military glamour with violence.[6] She was horrified by brutality towards the Indians, and nursed an Indian casually shot and left for dead in the woods.

In 1818 Phelan returned to Ireland; Charlotte followed, fearing life amidst savages. He sued the trustees of his estate, and was often in Dublin, leaving her alone copying legal documents. Charlotte took to religious brooding and experienced a classic Calvinist conversion experience. She composed tracts (as "Charlotte Elizabeth") for the Dublin-based Religious Tract Society; these provided finance and contact with the growing network of Evangelical "Saints". When her husband was transferred to Canada in 1820 she refused to accompany him. Tonna moved to Kilkenny, where a well-established Evangelical subculture centred on the Ossory Clerical Association, founded in 1800 by Hans Hamilton, Rector of

Knocktopher, Peter Roe, Minister of St Mary's (Kilkenny city), and Robert Shaw of St John's.[7]

Evangelicalism spread in the Church of Ireland amidst a wider reform movement; the organisational and intellectual weaknesses of Irish Catholicism were overestimated, encouraging hopes that concerted missionary action might win Ireland for Protestantism and loyalty. Several societies for popular education were influenced by Evangelicalism; in 1820 O'Connellite challenges led some of these bodies to proclaim their conversionist intentions. This provoked public debates between Protestant and Catholic spokesmen; at the Carlow meeting of 18–19 December 1824, four priests debated Evangelicals led by Robert Daly, future Bishop of Cashel.[8] Despite Tonna's optimistic view, it appears these proceedings provoked disturbances while confirming existing beliefs; the Carlow meeting ended with a riot and the flight of the Protestant speakers. The possibility that Evangelical conversionists might secure control of a state-supported educational system unless Catholic political influence could be strengthened aligned conservative Catholic elites with O'Connell.[9]

The years 1819–23 saw a major upsurge of agrarian violence (particularly in eastern Munster and southern Leinster). The "Rockite" movement was associated with popularisation of a commentary on the Book of Revelation, written by the English Catholic bishop Charles Walmesley ("Signor Pastorini"); Pastorini suggested the locusts from the Pit in Revelation 8 were the Protestant sects, which would disappear in 1825, three hundred years after Luther's defection. Tonna witnessed Rockite activities while staying at Knocktopher rectory.

In Kilkenny Tonna taught several deaf and dumb children, surreptitiously influencing them against Catholicism; one of these, John Britt, she regarded as her adopted son. Her description of their relationship is a reminder that one motive for the development of sign language by Catholic and Protestant educators was desire to bring the deaf and dumb to salvation.[10] (Shared interest in educating the deaf and dumb may explain the admiration expressed by the "Presbyterian laureate" William McComb, who wrote two poems in her honour.)[11]

In 1824 Captain Phelan resurfaced. He subsequently claimed her earnings as his property (the legal position until the 1882 Married Women's Property Act). Tonna left hurriedly for England and the protection of her brother. "Incipient derangement" kept Phelan from enforcing his claim until his death in 1837, but for some time she refused payment for her writings and received financial assistance from friends (including Lord Mountsandford, an elderly Roscommon evangelical landlord she saw as a father-figure; he proposed marriage after her husband's death). She left Ireland in tears. Like Anthony Trollope (whom she would have detested) she reshaped a troubled life in Ireland, and remained emotionally attached to the "land of my second birth".

Tonna lived for a year near Clifton, close to Hannah More, then shared her brother's household while he was stationed at Sandhurst. She became secretary of the Birmingham Female Anti-Slavery Society; she later recalled the anti-slavery movement as "a triumph of female chivalry" and urged women to boycott goods produced by sweated labour as abolitionist women boycotted slave produce.[12]

In 1828 Tonna's brother was posted to Ireland and drowned on Lough Owel. Tonna feared he might have died without a formal conversion experience, and been damned. She suffered a massive breakdown, ended only by anger at the onset of Catholic Emancipation. Revelation 13: 3 describes the Beast as having revived after suffering a mortal wound; Tonna saw the Wellington government's willingness to concede Catholic Emancipation rather than face full-scale civil war in Ireland as undoing the blow dealt against Antichrist at the Reformation, and the sight of Catholic MPs allowed "to legislate for the ordering of God's temple" and reducing the number of Irish Anglican bishoprics, made her think the "abomination of desolation" denounced in Daniel and Revelation had arisen at Westminster.

After John Britt's death from tuberculosis in 1830, Tonna moved to London. She undertook missionary work amongst Irish immigrants in the East End, becoming the archetypal figure of nineteenth-century Catholic fears, the female "Souper" combining charity with proselytism. Her hopes for mass conversion of Irish Catholics were kept alive by missionary societies which used the Irish language as a medium for conversion, recruiting Irish-speaking converts as lay evangelists.

As well as publishing moral tales (notably an account of the siege of Derry) Tonna entered Evangelical journalism, editing the *Christian Lady's Magazine* (1836–46), the *Protestant Magazine* (1841–4) and the 1840 *Protestant Annual.* She denounced Whig retrenchments on the Church of Ireland, and opening Irish municipal governments to Catholics as tyranny unparalleled since James II,[13] denounced the National Schools for being non-denominational, and called the Tithe War Popish persecution.

Some Anglican Evangelicals seceded to Nonconformity in response to Catholic Relief Act and "Romanising" tendencies within Anglicanism, represented by the Oxford Movement. Tonna maintained the Foxean vision of a covenanted nation, whose collective apostasy must be resisted collectively. She joined attempts to create a pan-Protestant Conservative alliance, uniting Evangelical Anglicans with nonconformists against further encroachment on the Protestant Constitution. Tonna associated with Henry Cooke, the Scottish Presbyterian leader Thomas Chalmers (whose political economics she thought too Malthusian and insufficiently Biblical)[14] and the Irish-born Liverpool cleric Hugh McNeile (1795–1879), son-in-law of Archbishop Magee of Dublin (who launched the Second Reformation in 1822). McNeile's belief that Protestant Ascendancy must be regained through Protestant democracy engendered the Liverpool tradition of populist Orange Toryism (and sectarian rioting).[15]

A tour of eastern and northern Ireland in 1837 (described in *Letters from Ireland*, addressed to her literary collaborator Lewis Hippolytus Joseph Tonna (1812–57))[16] moves through the social networks which drove the Second Reformation and Irish political Protestantism. She visited Vinegar Hill as a sacred site of Protestant martyrdom, and met a woman whose husband was piked in 1798;[17] she visited the aged Major Sirr. Sirr's antiquarian Irish-language interests encompassed evangelisation; she rejoiced that he strove for his country with the Word as formerly with his sword. They inspected his Achill amethysts and discussed Mr Nangle's Achill Mission. Tonna met "moral agents" employed by Lord Farnham and the millenarian Duke of Manchester to supervise tenants' moral and religious behaviour. She stayed with the leading Orange Evangelical Lord Roden at Tollymore, hailed him as embodying Protestant paternalism, and mourned the suppression of the Orange Order. She met Cooke in Belfast, accepting his historical corrections to her novel on the Siege of Derry; she had given him a ring inscribed NULLA PAX CUM ROMA.[18] She visited Derry, was unofficially enrolled as an Apprentice Boy, and insisted that only direct Divine intervention had preserved the city.

In 1841 she married the 29-year-old Lewis Tonna. This provoked comment; she claimed she determined on the marriage only after addressing God in prayer. Her latter years were dominated by campaigns for factory legislation and on behalf of the Jews. Her belief that God (and Satan) regularly intervened in earthly affairs was echoed by belief that the upper classes should intervene to protect the poor. Tonna attacked those postmillennialist providentialists who held that God governed the world through immutable economic laws.[19] She supported Shaftesbury's proposed factory legislation with one of the first English social novels, *Helen Fleetwood: A Tale of the Factories* and *The Perils of the Nation* (1843), a treatise criticising political economy through a mixture of Biblical literalism and paternalist rural nostalgia. (It appeared anonymously lest female authorship should diminish its influence.)

Her interest in the Jews, dating to her conversion, was intensified by Hugh McNeile's belief that the fulfilment of prophecy was at hand. Seeing the Sultan of Turkey as the

Eastern Antichrist, the Pope's Western counterpart, she believed Greek independence heralded the decline of his empire—the "drying up of the Euphrates" before the Battle of Armageddon (Revelation 16: 12–14). Literalism led her to reject the "spiritualising" view that Biblical prophecies of a new Jerusalem were fulfilled in the Christian Church; like many Evangelicals she expected that the Jews would soon return to Palestine and embrace Christianity. She supported missionary work among Jews, and welcomed the appointment of a Jewish convert as first Protestant Bishop of Jerusalem. In the early 1840s she disturbed Evangelicals by claiming the Old Covenant remained valid for Jews, and Jewish Christians should retain the Laws of Moses. Her outspoken denunciations of the persecution of Jews in Morocco, the Papal States and Russia won the respect and friendship of prominent Jews, including Sir Moses Montefiore and the journalist Jacob Franklin.[20] She gave up all forms of fiction as unreal diversions; her sensuous and imaginative side found expression through collecting medals and semi-precious stones and in the cultivation of a flower garden which doubled as a mnemonic aid (one of her books is structured around it).

Tonna suggested Ireland was mystically linked to the Jews, whom the Irish had never persecuted. Remoteness from Ireland sustained her hopes for the Second Reformation; she thought many nominal Catholics would soon declare themselves Protestants, and as England reverted to Roman apostasy a Protestant Ireland might provide refuge for the saints.[21] (Her acceptance of the unfounded rumour that the outspoken Catholic Bishop of Kildare and Leighlin, James Doyle, died a Protestant, reflects this wishful thinking.)[22]

In 1844 she developed inoperable cancer. Refusing opiates, she wrote to the end, assisted by an apparatus after her left hand was paralysed. She struggled to the first meeting of the Evangelical Alliance in January 1846. At the beginning of July she went to convalesce in Ramsgate as the guest of Sir Moses Montefiore; she was carried to the railway station, pronouncing a biblical curse upon the future Westminster Cathedral. At

Ramsgate she suffered a severe haemorrhage. With her last conscious breath she besought Jewish friends to accept Jesus as Messiah. "Her death took place on the ninth of Ab, when throughout the world the Jews were mourning the destruction of Jerusalem . . . it was also the anniversary of the Battle of the Boyne, the day when her room had always been decked with the choicest Orange lilies."[23] Her grave at Ramsgate was planted with shamrocks. Her husband came to see her death as a Divine mercy sparing her the worst horrors of the Famine besetting "her beloved Ireland", that famine which highlighted the failings of economic providentialism.

Personal Recollections

The present text abridges the central section of *Personal Recollections*, written in 1840 as a series of letters to Lewis Tonna and published in book form in 1841. Tonna's husband added an epilogue to the 1847 edition, not included here, which describes her last years and death. She presents herself as writing at his request, and emphasises that large sections of her life are off-limits; she forbids friends to assist biographers and destroys correspondence after the death of its author. She regrets the law of libel does not apply after death, when her policy may encourage unscrupulous invention which she cannot contradict. She is therefore obliged to describe

> that mental and spiritual discipline by which it has pleased the Lord to prepare me for the very humble, yet not very narrow, sphere of literary usefulness in which it was his good purpose to bid me move, with whatever of outward things, passing events, and individual personal adventure . . . may be needed to illustrate the progress . . . Into private domestic history no person possessed of a particle of delicacy can wish to intrude. Of living contemporaries I shall of course not speak; of the dead no farther than I would myself be spoken of by them, had I gone first. Public events I shall freely discuss, and hold back nothing that bears on spiritual affairs.

She denies egotism; those who make such accusations against autobiographers allow biographers to speculate where they are necessarily ignorant. (Some contemporary criticisms suggest an tendency to overdramatise; Roe's biographer, expressing repentance for attending a nun's profession from curiosity, rebukes Tonna for suggesting she was the only Kilkenny Protestant who stayed away.)[24]

The worldview of the opponents of Catholic Emancipation, uncongenial to later generations, has received relatively little attention. Tonna provides significant insights into the sense of siege felt by small Protestant communities during the agrarian violence of the 1820s, and shows how that experience reinforced wider narratives of Protestant endurance and martyrdom. (Tonna's vision of the siege of Derry as domestic drama was significantly influenced by her experiences at Knocktopher.) She provides interesting glimpses of Rockism, such as the link to hurling matches (violent participatory affairs involving huge crowds over miles of countryside, rather than the team-centred spectator sport produced by later codification). Tonna explains the coexistence of savage violence with surprising instances of restraint by calling rank-and- file Rockites reluctant tools of a ruthless conspiratorial elite; the contrast probably represented a "moral economy" of violence—crude and inconsistent attempts to distinguish legitimate and illegitimate targets.

Tonna's account of Rockism reflected an ongoing literary-political controversy. The liberal and pro-Catholic view, popularised by Thomas Moore's *Memoirs of Captain Rock* (1824) attributed Rockism to misgovernment, the absence of Catholic Emancipation and the financial exactions of the Church of Ireland. (Moore incidentally satirises Protestant missionaries.) *Captain Rock* stimulated numerous imitations from supporters and opponents; the latter (including Tonna in her novel *The Rockite*) accused Moore of trivialising Rockite violence, emphasised Pastorini's prophecies as proof of Catholic violence and ignorance, and attributed Rockism to a centrally directed Catholic conspiracy.[25] (Liberals played down Pastorini, emphasising Catholic elite opposition and even attributing the craze to Anti-Emancipationists seeking to discredit Catholicism; an upsurge in peasant demand for Bibles from evangelists was partly due to Catholic prophecy believers seeking to confirm Pastorini from Revelation.) Tonna's belief in direct angelic and demonic intervention in human affairs predisposed her to see conscious design; for her, the peasant shooting his land-lord is linked directly to the Vatican and thence to Satan.[26] Her presentation of Moore as a conscious conspirator, killing more with his verse than any peasant with his pike, is a reminder that later indictments of Moore as lachrymose West British social climber forget the contemporary political charge his writings carried.

Tonna's view is self-sealing; once it is assumed that the Catholic Church is behind Rockism, Catholic victims are explained away since anyone who opposes Rockism is seen as an enemy of the Church. Other terms of reference are auto-matically excluded; the Marum murder, which she describes at length, was cited by liberals to support the agrarian inter-pretation of Rockism, since it prevented Marum buying out an insolvent Protestant landlord. (The Catholic tenants preferred an established landlord to an ambitious grazier, seeking increased economic returns at their expense.)[27] Her views contained just enough truth to make them seem plausible; recent scholarship suggests that although Rockism was primarily agrarian, millennial expectations gave it unusual cohesion and determination, and it did possess rudimentary central leadership.[28]

Linda Peterson argues that Tonna's autobiography is primarily a defence against charges of unfeminine behaviour. She does not describe her writings in detail (she may assume readers' acquaintance with them), presents her marriage break-up as sent by God to test her spirit, and treats her career as both a divinely imposed mission and an extension of domesticity.[29] She presents women's role in the Protestant cause in terms of the strong-hearted wives of Foxe's martyrs, assisting their husbands' sacrifice (although Foxe describes female as well as male martyrs). Linda Colley points out that the last-ditch British petitions against Catholic Emancipation produced the most widespread female political intervention hitherto seen in British history; some Emancipationists ridiculed this "unfeminine" display, while anti-Emancipationists deployed the gendered argument used by Tonna—that Catholicism threatened domesticity, which women must defend.[30] Tonna's account of her activities reflects this campaign and its limitations. Her Biblical exemplar, the prophetess Deborah, nerved the Hebrew general Barak by assuring him of divine favour but could not act without him;[31] Tonna organised the petition but did not circulate or sign it herself, and emphasises that only men signed. (The limitation of the prophetess as feminine exemplar is that her inspiration, coming directly from God, is an exception which cannot be generalised; Tonna criticises the proto-Pentecostal Irvingites for violating St Paul's prohibition on women teaching men by incorporating the utterances of "prophetesses" into formal church services.)

Her principal contemporary exemplar is Hannah More, whom she also compares to Deborah. More serves as a role-model through her career as a professional religious writer, her attempts to counter political subversion through charitable education and cheap loyalist tracts, and her excoriation by somnolent High Churchmen who denounced the "Queen of the Methodists" for encouraging nonconformity and undertaking tasks reserved for her "natural" superiors. (The "slander" mentioned by Tonna was an insinuation that an annuity provided for More by a former fiancé rewarded sexual favours; perhaps Tonna feared her own relations with patrons might incur similar misrepresentations.) The sufferings of More's old age—she outlived her sisters and was robbed by trusted servants—reinforce Tonna's view that the Lord's servants must expect suffering and ingratitude.[32]

Hannah More held a rationalistic Evangelicalism reflecting the postmillennialist view that worldwide diffusion of Christianity would produce a thousand years of peace, faith and prosperity before the trials of the Last Days and Second Coming.[33] Tonna believed the earth had been created in 4004 BC and would literally last seven thousand years, mirroring the seven days of creation with the Millennium as Sabbath; her Irish experiences made her feel Revelation's portrayal of persecution more immediately relevant than postmillennialism suggested. Hugh McNeile encouraged her, among other younger Evangelicals, to see contemporary upheavals confirming premillennialism; the coming of Antichrist and final persecution would precede the millennium, and Jesus would rule a regenerate earth for a thousand years before the Last Judgment. (Historically the dominant Christian view is anti-literalist Augustinian amillennialism, where the millennium symbolises the Church throughout history.)[34]

McNeile's views were influenced by Presbyterian preacher Edward Irving (1792–1834) and the Evangelical banker Henry Drummond (1786–1860), who organised conferences on prophecy 1826–30 at Drummond's Surrey mansion. Similar conferences at Powerscourt, County Wicklow 1831–3 involved the discontented Church of Ireland cleric John Nelson Darby (1800–82). Tonna and McNeile came to believe Irving's confused attempts to emphasise the humanity of Jesus compromised His Divinity; evangelicals were further embarrassed when Irving and Drummond were led by apocalypticism to hail hysterical "speaking in tongues" amongst Irving's congregation as reviving apostolic prophecy.

Tonna saw the Irvingite debacle as further proof of Satan redoubling his efforts to deceive the elect. Her only encounter with Daniel O'Connell, at an April 1832 meeting of the Anti-Slavery Society, was experienced from this perspective. (Ironically, O'Connell's speech defended women's right to petition.)[35] She thinks O'Connell, like Satan, too dangerous to be treated as a figure of fun; she presents him, like Napoleon, as a scourge unleashed by God to punish apostasy.

Irving and Drummond formed their own "Catholic Apostolic Church". Darby also left Anglicanism to found the "Brethren"; through his widely disseminated version of premillennialism the last-ditch Evangelical defence of the Protestant Constitution influenced twentieth-century American Protestant Fundamentalism. (Darby's "futurist" view—of Biblical prophecies as fulfilled in "prophetic time", pausing at Pentecost but resuming when the saints were raptured to Heaven before the tribulation—proved more flexible, and more alluring, than the "historicist" view that the prophecies operated in ordinary time and saints must suffer with the rest.)[36]

Tonna, like More, is a deeply equivocal figure. She overcame financial hardship and marital strife to become a successful journalist and writer; she asserted her autonomous agency through advocating fanatical conservatism and biblical literalism. Her limited defences of women's political and social activism anticipate features of nineteenth-century feminism; yet despite her unhappy experiences she advocated a literally patriarchal society. She genuinely sought the spiritual and material welfare of various out-groups—Jews, Irish peasants, factory workers—incurring considerable trouble and unpopularity on their behalf; her worldview consigned them to perpetual legal childhood as an extension of their landlord's family. They could not call their souls their own; Tonna expressly argued that householders with a dying Catholic servant or guest were obliged to refuse access to a Catholic priest or be cursed for facilitating idolatry. She came to detest the glamorisation of military life and argue that only defensive warfare was justified; yet she frequently expresses Christianity through martial imagery, the officer—private relationship recurs as model of paternalism, and her Sandhurst missionary activities contributed to the stern military evangelicalism which drove many mid-Victorian colonial campaigns.

Some commentators read *Personal Recollections* as the work of a masochistic collaborator with patriarchal oppression;[37] it may be seen instead as the attempt of a clever, imaginative person to impose order on a troubled and confusing world. She made sense of suffering and loss as God's will, excising parts of her sensibility which threatened her project of self-definition. She felt an impulse to dance at the St John's

Eve bonfire, but on reflection condemned it as worshipping Moloch.

"So poor 'Charlotte Eliz.' is dead" commented her Unitarian fellow-townswoman Harriet Martineau. "How amazed she will be yonder at finding that she could be mistaken!"[38]

NOTES

1   The version of her name in the *Dictionary of National Biography*.

2   Linda Colley, *Britons: Forging the Nation 1707–1837* (London, 1992).

3   Tonna, *Passing Thoughts* (London, 1838).

4   Mary Prior Hack, *Consecrated Women* (London, 1882), pp. 73–124.

5   Virginia Blain, Isobel Grundy and Patricia Clements (eds), *Feminist Companion to Literature in English* (New Haven CT, 1990), p. 1987.

6   Clare Midgley, *Women against Slavery: The British Campaigners 1780–1870* (London, 1992), pp. 58, 99. The poem circulated with "The British Slave" by Hannah More.

7   Samuel Madden *Memoir of the Life of the Late Reverend Peter Roe* (Dublin, 1842); I owe this reference to Gary Owens. For a sceptical view of Roe which argues that corrupt eighteenth-century clerics were better rounded than their reforming successors, see Hubert Butler "The Bishop" in *Escape From the Anthill* (Mullingar, 1986), pp. 32–45.

8   Desmond Bowen, *The Protestant Crusade in Ireland 1800-70* (Dublin, 1978); Stewart J. Brown, "The New Reformation Movement in the Church of Ireland, 1801–29" in Stewart J. Brown and David W. Miller (eds), *Piety and Power in Ireland 1790–1960: Essays in Honour of Emmet Larkin* (Belfast and Notre Dame, 2000), pp. 180–208.

9   Irene Whelan "The stigma of Souperism" in Cathal Poirteir (ed.), *The Great Irish Famine* (Cork, 1995), pp. 135–54.

10 Tonna *Memoir of John Britt* (London, 1854).

11 For McComb see William McComb, *The Repealer Repulsed*, ed. Patrick Maume (Dublin, 2003).

12 Midgley, *Women Against Slavery*; Tonna, *Perils of the Nation* (London, 1843).

13 Tonna *The Flower Garden* (London, 1840).

14 *Perils of the Nation*, pp. 178, 183.

15 Frank Neal, *Sectarian Violence: The Liverpool Experience* (Manchester, 1988), pp. 44–52. See also McNeile's DNB entry.

16 Tonna, *Letters from Ireland* (London, 1838), pp. 340–1.

17 Tonna, *Flower Garden*.

18 J. L. Porter *Life And Times of Rev. Henry Cooke* (Belfast, 1871, new edn, 1875), pp. 227–39; J. S. Reid *History of the Presbyterian Church in Ireland* (new edn, Belfast, 1867), pp. ii, 353 n16; 375–6 n52; Tonna, *Letters from Ireland*, pp. 340–1.

19 Boyd Hilton *The Age of Atonement: The Influence of Evangelicalism on Social and Economic Thought, 1765–1865)* (Oxford, 1988), pp. 10–11, 94–8, 211–12, 380–1.

20 William D. Rubinstein and Hilary L. Rubinstein, *Philosemitism: Admiration and Support in the English-Speaking World for Jews, 1840–1939* (London, 1999); Lewis Tonna's postscript to the 1847 edn of *Personal Recollections*; Nadia Valman "Women writers and the campaign for Jewish civil rights in early Victorian England" in Kathryn Gleadle and Sarah Richardson (eds), *Women in British Politics, 1760–1860: The Power of the Petticoat* (Basingstoke, 2000).

21 Tonna, *Second Causes* (London, 1842).

22 Bowen, *Protestant Crusade*, p. 102.

23 *Personal Recollections* (1847 edn), pp. 429–30.

24 Madden, *Peter Roe*, p. 412.

25 Luke Gibbons, "Between Captain Rock and a hard place: art and agrarian insurgency" in Timothy Foley and Sean Ryder (eds), *Ideology and Ireland in the Nineteenth Century* (Dublin, 1998); Joep Leerssen, *Remembrance and Imagination* (Cork, 1996), pp. 82–8.

26 Tonna, preface to 6th (revised) edn of *Derry* (1836).

27 James S. Donnelly Jr "Pastorini and Captain Rock: Millenarianism and Sectarianism in the Rockite Movement of 1821–4" in Samuel Clark and James S. Donnelly (eds), *Irish Peasants: Violence and Political Unrest 1780–1914* (Manchester, 1983), pp. 102–39.

28 Sean J. Connolly "Mass politics and sectarian conflict 1823–30" in W. E. Vaughan (ed.) *A New History of Ireland*, vol. VI: 1801–70 (Oxford, 1989), pp. 74–107.

29 Linda H. Peterson, *Traditions of Victorian Women's Autobiography: The Poetics and Politics of Life Writing* (Charlottesville, VA, 1999).

30 Colley, *Britons*, pp. 329–34; Clare Midgley "From supporting missions to petitioning parliament: women and the evangelical campaign against *Sati* in India, 1813–30" in Gleadle and Richardson (eds), *Women in British Politics, 1760–1860*; Midgley, *Women Against Slavery*.

31 For Deborah as awkward Evangelical exemplar see Andrea Ebel Brozyna, *Labour, Love and Prayer: Female Piety in Ulster Religious Literature 1850–1914* (Belfast, 1999), p. 96.

32 Anne Stott, *Hannah More: The First Victorian* (Oxford, 2003); Colley, *Britons*.

33 Hilton *Age of Atonement*, pp. 207, 380–1; Stott, *Hannah More*, pp. 319–20.

34 Roe's amillennialism is discussed in Madden, *Memoir of Rev. Peter Roe*, pp. 438–45.

35 Midgley, *Women Against Slavery*, p. 64.

36 Paul Boyer, *When Time Shall Be No More: Prophecy Belief in Modern American Culture* (Cambridge, Mass., 1992).

37 Peterson, *Traditions of Victorian Women's Autobiography* p. 62, drawing on the views of Elizabeth Kowalski; Mark McGovern "We have a strong city: politicised Protestantism, evangelicalism and the siege myth in early nineteenth-century Derry" in William Kelly (ed.), *The Sieges of Derry* (Dublin, 2001).

38 Quoted in Peterson, *Traditions of Victorian Women's Autobiography*, p. 59.

NOTE ON THE TEXT

Irish Recollections is an abridged version of the 1841 edition of *Personal Recollections*. The original spelling and punctuation have been retained, with very minor modifications made for clarity. Cuts in the text are marked with three asterisks * * *

Thanks to Paul Bew, Enda Delaney, Gary Owens, Nini Rodgers, Hilary Rubinstein and participants in the 1999 conference of the Society for the Study of Nineteenth-Century Ireland.

IRISH RECOLLECTIONS

PERSONAL RECOLLECTIONS

OF

Charlotte Elizabeth.

SEELEY, JACKSON & HALLIDAY,

FLEET STREET, LONDON.

LETTER V.

IRELAND.

I now arrive at an epoch from which I may date the commencement of all that deserves to be called life, inasmuch as I had hitherto been living without God in the world. My existence was a feverish dream, of vain pleasures first, and then of agitations and horrors. My mind was a chaos of useless information, my character of unapplied energies, my heart a waste of unclaimed affections, and my hope an enigma of confused speculations. I had plenty to do, yet felt that I was doing nothing; and there was a glowing want within my bosom, a craving after I knew not what; a restless, unsatisfied, unhappy feeling, that seemed in quest of some unknown good. How this was awakened, I know not: it was unaccompanied with any conviction of my own sinfulness, or any doubt of my perfect safety as a child of God. I did not anticipate any satisfaction from change of place; but readily prepared to obey a summons from my husband to follow him to Ireland, whither he had gone to engage in a law-suit. To be sure I hated Ireland most cordially; I had never seen it, and as a matter of choice would have preferred New South Wales, so completely was I influenced by the prevailing prejudice against that land of barbarism! Many people despise Ireland, who, if you demand a reason, will tell you it is a horrid place, and the people all savages; but if you press for proofs and illustrations, furthermore such deponents say not.

On a dull day in April I took my place, a solitary traveller, in the Shrewsbury coach, quite ignorant as to the road I was to travel, and far less at home than I should have been in the wildest part of North America, or on the deck of a ship bound to circumnavigate the globe. We rattled out of London, and the first thing that at all aroused my attention was a moon-light view of Oxford, where we stopped at midnight to change horses. Those old grey towers, and mighty masses of ancient building, on which the silvery ray fell with fine effect, awoke in my bosom two melancholy trains of thought; one was the recollection of my father, whose enthusiastic attachment to his own university had often provoked warm discussion with the no less attached Cantabs of our old social parties; and who had often held out to me, as the greatest of earthly gratifi-cations, a visit with him to that seat of learning, which he would describe in glowing colours. But where was my father now? His poor girl, the delight of his eyes and treasure of his heart, was in Oxford, with none to guide, none to guard, none to speak a cheering word to her. I shrank back in the coach; and grieved over this till a sudden turning once more threw before me the outline of some magnificent old fabric, bathed in moonlight, and that called up a fit of patriotism, calculated to darken yet more the prospect before me. This was England, my own proud England; and these the "cloud-capped towers, the gorgeous palaces," that distinguished her seats of learning above all others. I was bound—for Ireland! What English young lady had ever studied the history of that remote, half-civilized settlement, called Ireland? Not I, cer-tainly, nor any of my acquaintance; but I took it for granted that Ireland had no antiquities, nothing to distinguish her from other barbarous lands, except that her people ate potatoes, made blunders, and went to mass. I felt it a sort of degra-dation to have an Irish name, and to go there as a resident; but comforted myself by resolving never in any particular to give into any Irish mode of living, speaking, or thinking, and to associate only with such as had been at least educated in England.

The next day's rising sun shone upon Stratford-on-Avon; and here revived in some degree, my Shakespearian mania, to the still higher exaltation of my English stilts, and the deeper debasement of all "rough Irish kernes." At Shrewsbury, we parted with a kind old lady, who had shown me some good-natured attentions; and I was left with only an elderly gentleman bound also for Dublin, who told me we must start at three o'clock on Sunday morning for Holyhead. I was dreadfully dejected, and told him I hoped he would not think the worse of me for being so utterly alone, and that he would excuse my retiring to my own apartment the instant we had dined. He took pencil and paper, and with a glow of benevolent feeling expressed his anxious desire to take the same care of me that he would of his own daughter, and to look on me as his special charge, until he should give me into the hands of my lawful protector. I thanked him with true English reserve, and a coldness that seemed rather to grate on his warm feelings; and having owned that his seeing my Newfoundland dog well fed and lodged would be a great obligation, I withdrew to fret alone over my exile to this foreign land. You may call this an exaggeration, but it is no such thing. I delight in dwelling upon my reluctant approach to the land that I was to love so fondly.

Next day my miseries were alleviated by the enchanting beauties of the Welsh country through which we passed; and my regard for Mr. D. greatly increased by the compassionate care he took of a poor sickly woman and her ragged infant, whom he descried on the top of the coach, and first threw his large cloak to them, then, with my cordial assent, took them inside, and watched them most kindly, until he fell asleep. I peeped into his fine benevolent face, and inwardly confessed there must be some nice people in Ireland.

At the inn where we dined, I made another acquaintance: a younger, but middle-aged man, whose vivacity, combined with Welch mutton and ale, quite raised my spirits. Hearing from Mr. D. with what enthusiasm I had admired the scenery of Llangollen, he volunteered to hand me in, at the coach-window, a note of every remarkable place we should approach during the rest of our journey, adding, "I know the road pretty well, having traversed it at least twice a year for sixteen years, passing to and from my Irish home." He was a legal man, a finished gentleman, and another sad drawback on my perverse prejudices. Mr. F. proved an excellent descriptive guide, punctually reaching to me from the roof of the coach his little memoranda, in time for me to take a survey of the object concerned; and also most assiduously aiding in the care of my luggage and dog, when we were all put into the ferry-boat.

There was then no bridge over the Menai, and I being in total ignorance of the route, was not a little dismayed at the embarkation; forgetting that Holyhead was in Anglesea, and that Anglesea was an island. At last, then the boat pushed off, the opposite shore being hidden under the midst of deepening twilight, I addressed the ferryman in a tone of remonstrance that infinitely diverted the whole party,

"Surely you are not going to take me over in this way to Ireland!"

"No, no," said Mr. F., "you shall have a good night's rest, and a better sea-boat, before we start for the dear green isle."

Steamers were not then upon the packet-station, and the wind being unfavourable, we had a passage of seventeen hours, not landing until two in the morning of Easter Sunday. Nothing could exceed my discomfort; as you may suppose, when I tell you that after paying my bill at Holyhead, I, in a fit of abstraction, deposited it very safely in my purse and in its stead threw away my last bank-note. The mistake was not suspected until, in mid-voyage, I examined the state of my finances, and found the sum total to amount to one shilling. This was an awful discovery! my passage was paid, but how to reach Dublin was a mystery, and such was the untamed pride of my character, that I would sooner have walked there than confessed to the fact, which might have been doubted, and laid myself under the obligation of a loan which I was sure of repaying in a few hours, even to good old Mr. D. When I stepped from the deck of the packet upon the plank that rested against the pier of Howth, I had not one single halfpenny in my pocket; and I experienced without the slightest emotion, one of the most hairbreadth escapes of my life.

The water was very low: the plank, of course, sloped greatly, and, as soon as I set my foot on it, began to slide down. In another second I should have been plunged between the vessel's side and the stone-pier, without any human possibility of rescue; and already I had lost my balance, when a sailor springing on the bulwarks, caught me round the knees, and at the same instant, Mr. F. throwing himself on the ground, seized and steadied the plank, until I recovered my footing and ran up. I shudder to recall the hardened indifference of my own spirit while the kind, warm-hearted Irishmen were agitated with strong emotion, and all around me thanking God for my escape. Each of my friends thought I had landed under the care of the other; while one had my dog, and the other my portmanteau. I received their fervent "cead-mille failthe" with cold politeness, and trod with feelings of disgust on the dear little green shamrocks that I now prize beyond gems.

We went to the hotel, and Mr. D. proposed my retiring to a chamber until the coach started; but my empty purse would not allow of that, so I said I preferred sitting where I was. Refreshments were ordered; but though in a state of ravenous hunger, I steadily refused to touch them; for I would not have allowed another person to pay for me, and was resolved to conceal my loss as long as I could. I was excused, on the presumption of a qualmishness resulting from the tossing of the ship; and most melancholy, most forlorn were the feelings with which I watched through the large window the fading moonbeams and the dawning day. To my unspeakable joy, the two proposed taking a post-chaise with me to Dublin, the expense being no more, and the comfort much greater than going by coach; and having requested Mr. F. to keep an exact account of my share in the charges, I took my seat beside them with a far lighter heart, my dog being on the foot-board in front of the carriage.

Away we drove, our horses young, fresh and in high condition. It was a glorious morning, and vainly did I strive not to admire the scenery, as one after another of the beautiful villas that adorn the Howth road gleamed out in the snowy whiteness that characterizes the houses there; generally embosomed in trees, and surrounded by gardens, on the rising grounds. We were descending the hilly road very rapidly, when by some means the horses took fright, and broke into full gallop, crossing and recrossing the road in a fearful manner. The driver was thrown on the foot-board, poor Tejo hung by his chain against the horses' legs, and our situation was most critical. I had suffered from one upset in America, and resolved not to encounter another; so quietly gathering my long riding-habit about me with one hand, and putting the other out at the window, I opened the door, and with one active spring flung myself out. You know the extreme peril, the almost certain destruction of such a leap from a carriage at full speed; I did not, or certainly I would not have taken it. However at that very instant of time the horses made a dead stop; and the chaise remained stationary only a few paces in advance of me.

Was not the hand of God here? Oh, surely it was, in the most marked and wonderful manner. No cause could be assigned for the arrest of the animals; the driver had lost the reins, and no one was near. I had fallen flat on the road side. just grazing my gloves with the gravel, and getting a good mouthful of the soil, with which my face was brought into involuntary contact. In a moment I sprang to my feet, and blowing it out, exclaimed with a laugh, "Oh well! I suppose I am to love this country after all; for I have kissed it in spite of me." I then ran to help my dog out of his disagreeable state of suspension, and returned to my friends, who were frightened and angry too, and who refused to let me into the chaise unless I positively promised not to jump out any more. To shorten the tale, I reached the Hibernian Hotel, where my husband was, seized some money, and paid my expenses without any one having discovered that I was a complete bankrupt up to that minute.

I have been very prolix here; for I cannot overlook a single incident connected with this eventful journey. Never did any one less anticipate a blessing, or look for happiness, than I did in visiting Ireland. I cannot enter into more particulars, because it would involve the names of friends who might not wish to figure in print; but if these pages ever meet the eyes of any who gave me the first day's welcome in Dublin, let them be assured that the remembrance of their tender kindness, the glowing warmth of their open hospitality, and their solicitude to make the poor stranger happy among them, broke through the ice of a heart that had frozen itself up in most unnatural reserve, and gave life to the first pulse that played within it, of the love that soon pervaded its every vein—the love of dear generous Ireland.

My first journey into the interior was to the King's County, where I passed some weeks in a house most curiously situated, with an open prospect of ten miles pure bog in front of it. Being newly built, nothing had yet had time to grow; but its owner, one of the most delightful old gentlemen I ever met with, had spared no cost to render it commodious and handsome. He was a fine specimen of the hospitable Irish gentlemen, and took great pleasure in bringing me acquainted with the customs of a people, and the features of a place, so new to me. Indeed, it was my first introduction to what was really Irish, for Dublin is too much of a capital city to afford many specimens of distinct nationality. On that great festival of the peasantry, St. John's eve, Mr. C. resolved on giving his tenants and neighbours a treat that should also enlighten me on one of the most singular relics of paganism. It is the custom at sunset on that evening to kindle numerous immense fires throughout the country, built like our bonfires, to a great height, the pile being composed of turf, bog-wood, and such other combustibles as they can gather. The turf yields a steady, substantial body of fire, the bog-wood a most brilliant flame; and the effect of these great beacons blazing on every hill, sending up volumes of smoke from every point of the horizon, is very remarkable. Ours was a magnificent one, being provided by the landlord as a compliment to his people, and was built on the lawn, as close beside the house as safety would admit. Early in the evening the peasants began to assemble, all habited in their best array, glowing with health, every countenance full of that sparkling animation and excess of enjoyment that characterize the enthusiastic people of the land. I had never seen anything resembling it, and was exceedingly delighted with their handsome, intelligent, merry faces; the bold bearing of the men, and the playful, but really modest deportment of the maidens; the vivacity of the aged people, and wild glee of the children. The fire being kindled, a splendid blaze shot up, and for a while they stood contemplating it, with faces strangely disfigured by the peculiar light first emitted when bogwood is thrown on: after a short pause, the ground was cleared in front of an old blind piper, the very *beau ideal* of energy, drollery, and shrewdness, who, seated on a low chair, with a well-plenished jug within his reach, screwed his pipes to the liveliest times and the endless jig began.

An Irish jig is interminable, so long as the party holds together; for when one of the dancers becomes fatigued, a fresh individual is ready to step into the vacated place quick as thought; so that the other does not pause, until in like manner obliged to give place to a successor. They continue footing it, and setting to one another, occasionally moving in a figure, and changing places with extraordinary rapidity, spirit and grace. Few indeed, among even the very lowest of the most impoverished class, have grown into youth without obtaining some lessons in this accomplishment from the travelling dancing-masters of their district; and certainly in the way they use it, many would be disposed to grant a dispensation to the young peasant which they would withhold from the young peer. It is, however, sadly abused among them, to sabbath-breaking, revellings, and the most immoral scenes, where they are congregated and kept together under its influence; and the same scene, enacted a year afterwards, would have awoke in my mind very different feelings from those with which I regarded this first spectacle of Irish hilarity; when I could hardly be restrained by the laughing remonstrances of "the quality" from throwing myself in the midst of the joyous group, and dancing with them.

But something was to follow that puzzled me not a little: when the fire had burned for some hours, and got low, an indispensable part of the ceremony commenced. Every one present of the peasantry passed through it, and several children were thrown across the sparkling embers; while a wooden frame of some eight feet long, with a horse's head fixed to one end, and a large white sheet thrown over it, concealing the wood and the man on whose head it was carried, made its appearance. This was greeted with loud shouts as the "white horse;" and having been safely carried by the skill of the bearer several times through the fire with a bold leap, it pursued the people, who ran screaming and laughing in every direction. I asked what the horse was meant for, and was told it represented all cattle. Here was the old pagan worship of Baal, if not of Moloch too, carried on openly and universally in the heart of a nominally Christian country, and by millions professing the christian name! I was confounded, for I did not then know that Popery is only a crafty adaptation of Pagan idolatries to its own scheme; and while I looked upon the now wildly-excited people with their children, and, in a figure, all their cattle, passing again and again through the fire, I almost questioned in my own mind the lawfulness of the spectacle, considered in the light that the Bible must, even to the natural heart, exhibit it in, to those who confess the true God. There was no one to whom I could breathe such thoughts, and they soon faded from my mind: not so the impression made on it by this fair specimen of a population whom I had long classed with the savage inhabitants of barbarous lands, picturing them to myself as dark, ferocious, discontented and malignant. That such was the reverse of their natural character I now began to feel convinced; and from that evening my heart gradually warmed towards a race whom I found to be frank, warm, and affectionate, beyond any I had ever met with.

My interest in them, however, was soon to be placed on another and a firmer basis. I took up my permanent abode in a neighbouring county; and within six months after that celebration of St. John's eve, I experienced the mighty power of God in a way truly marvellous. Great and marvellous are *all* his works; in creating, in sustaining, in governing this world of wonderful creatures; but oh, how surprisingly marvellous and great in redeeming lost sinners; in taking away the heart of stone, and giving a heart of flesh, and making his people willing in the day of his power! I have carefully abstained from any particulars respecting myself that could either cast a reproach on the dead or give pain to the living! I shall do so still, and merely remark that, as far as this world was concerned, my lot had no happiness mingled in it, and that my only solace under many grievous trials consisted in two things: one was a careful concealment of whatever might subject my proud spirit to the mortification of being pitied when I desired rather to be envied; and the other a confident assurance that in suffering afflictions silently, unresistingly and uncomplainingly, I was making God my debtor to a large amount. What desperate wickedness of a deceived and deceitful heart was this? The very thing in which I so arrogantly vaunted myself before God was the direct result of personal pride, in itself a great sin; and thus I truly gloried in my shame. I never looked beyond the rod to Him who had appointed it; but satisfying myself that I had not merited, from man, any severity, my demerits at the hand of the Most High were wholly put out of the calculation. Thus, of course, every stroke drove me further from the only Rock of refuge, and deeper into the fastnesses of my own vain conceits. Added to this, I was wholly shut out from all the ordinary means by which the Lord usually calls sinners to himself. There was no gospel ministry then within my reach; nor could I, if it were provided, have profited by it, owing to my infirmity. Into Christian society I had never entered; nor had the least glimmer of spiritual light shone into my mind. My religion was that of the Pharisee, and my addresses to God included, like his, an acknowledgment that it was by divine favour I was so much better than my neighbours. Reality had so far chased away romance, that my old favourite authors had little power to charm me; and the hollowness of my affected gaiety and ease made society a very sickening thing. Besides, at my first coming to the very aristocratical little town where I then resided, I was neglected in a manner very mortifying to one who had been accustomed to find her level in society even a grade higher than that; and this was most mercifully ordered, not only to humble my intolerable pride, but to smooth the way for that separation from worldly associates which was soon to become the desire of my heart; and to aid me in afterwards withstanding the temptation of most earnest and affectionate attentions from all around me, when, by means of an old friend very high indeed in military command, my real standing in society became better known to them.

At the time I am now speaking of, I was living in perfect seclusion, and uninterrupted solitude. Captain P. was always in Dublin, and my chief occupation was in hunting out, and transcribing and arranging matter for the professional gentlemen conducting the law-suit, from a mass of confused family papers and documents. Our property consisted of a large quantity of poor cabins, with their adjoining land, forming a complete street on the outskirts of the town, which was greatly in arrear to the head-landlords, and a periodical "distress" took place. On these occasions, a keeper was set over the property; some legal papers were served, and all the household goods, consisting of iron kettles, wooden stools, broken tables, a ragged blanket or two, and the little stores of potatoes, the sole support of the wretched inhabitants, were brought out, piled in a long row down the street, and "canted," that is, put up for sale, for the payment of perhaps, one or two per cent, of the arrears. This horrified me beyond measure: I was ashamed to be seen among the people who were called our tenants, though this proceeding did not emanate from their immediate landlord; and every thing combined to render the seclusion of my own garden more congenial to me than any wider range.

It was then that I came to the resolution of being a perfect devotee in religion; I thought myself marvellously good; but something of a monastic mania seized me. I determined to emulate the recluses of whom I had often read; to become a sort of Protestant nun; and to fancy my garden, with its high stone-walls, and little thicket of apple-trees, a convent-enclosure. I also settled it with myself to pray three or four times every day, instead of twice; and with great alacrity entered upon this new routine of devotion.

Here God met with, and arrested me. When I kneeled down to pray, the strangest alarms took hold of my mind. He to whom I had been accustomed to prate with flippant volubility in a set form of heartless words seemed to my startled mind so exceedingly terrible in unapproachable majesty, and so very angry with me in particular, that I became paralyzed with fear. I strove against this, with characteristic pertinacity: I called to mind all the common-place assurances respecting the sufficiency of a good intention, and magnified alike my doings and my sufferings. I persuaded myself it was only a holy awe, the effect of distinguished piety and rare humility, and that I was really an object of the divine complacency in no ordinary degree. Again I essayed to pray, but in vain; I dared not. Then I attributed it to a nervous state of feeling which would wear away by a little abstraction from the subject; but this would not do. To leave off praying was impossible, yet to pray seemed equally so. I well remember that the character in which I chiefly viewed the Lord God was that of an Avenger, going forth to smite the first-born of Egypt; and I somehow identified myself with the condemned number. Often, after kneeling a long time, I have laid my face upon my arms, and wept most bitterly because I could not, dared not pray.

It was not in my nature to be driven back easily from any path I had entered on; and here the Lord wrought upon me to persevere resolutely. I began to examine myself, in order to discover *why* I was afraid, and taking as my rule the ten commandments, I found myself sadly deficient on some points. The tenth affected me as it had never had done before. "I had not known lust," because I had not understood the law when it said "Thou shalt not covet." A casual glance at the declaration of St. James, "Whosoever shall keep the whole law, and yet offend in one point, he is guilty of all," alarmed me exceedingly; and on a sudden it occurred to me, that not only the ten commandments, but all the precepts of the New Testament, were binding on a Christian; and I trembled more than ever.

What was to be done? To reform myself, certainly, and become obedient to the whole law. Accordingly I went to work, transcribed all the commands that I felt myself most in the habit of neglecting, and pinned up a dozen or two of texts round my room. It required no small effort to enter this apartment and walk round it, reading my mementos. The active schoolmaster, the law, had got me fairly under his rod, and dreadful were the writhings of the convicted culprit! I soon, however, took down my texts fearing lest anyone might see them, and not knowing they were for myself, be exasperated. I then made a little book, wrote down a list of offences, and commenced making a dot over against each, whenever I detected myself in the commission of one. I had become very watchful over my thoughts, and was honest in recording all evil; so my book became a mass of black dots; and the reflection that occurred to me of omissions also being sins, completed the panic of my mind. I flung my book into the fire, and sank into an abyss of gloomy despair.

How long this miserable state of mind lasted, I do not exactly remember: I think about two weeks. I could not pray. I dared not read the Bible, it bore so very hard upon me. Outwardly I was calm and even cheerful, but within reigned the very blackness of darkness. Death, with which I had so often sported, appeared in my eyes so terrible, that the slightest feeling of illness filled my soul with dismay. I saw no way of escape: I had God's perfect law before my eyes, and a full conviction of my own past sinfulness and present helplessness, leaving me wholly without hope. Hitherto I had never known a day's illness for years; one of God's rich mercies to me consisted in uninterrupted health, and a wonderful freedom from all nervous affections. I knew as almost little of the sensation of a headache as I did of that of tight lacing; and now a violent cold, with sore throat, aggravated into fever by the state of my mind, completely prostrated me. I laid myself down on the sofa one morning, and waited to see how my earthly miseries would terminate; too well knowing what must follow the close of a sinner's life.

I had not lain long, when a neighbour, hearing I was ill, sent me some books, just received from Dublin, as a loan, hoping I might find some amusement in them. Listlessly, wretchedly, mechanically, I opened one—it was the memoir of a departed son, written by his father. I read a page, describing the approach of death, and was arrested by the youth's expressions of self-condemnation, his humble acknowledgement of having deserved at the Lord's hand nothing but eternal death. "Ah, poor fellow," said I, "he was like me. How dreadful his end must have been! I will see what he said at last, when on the very brink of the bottomless pit." I resumed the book; and found him in continuation glorifying God that though *he* was so guilty and so vile, there was One able to save to the uttermost, who had borne his sins, satisfied divine justice for him, opened the gates of heaven, and now waited to receive his ransomed soul.

The book dropped from my hands. "Oh, what is this? This is what I want: this would save me—Who did this for him? Jesus Christ, certainly; and it must be written in the New Testament." I tried to jump up and reach my Bible, but was overpowered by the emotion of my mind. I clasped my hands over my eyes, and then the blessed effects of having even a literal knowledge of Scripture was apparent. Memory brought before me, as the Holy Spirit directed it, not here and there a detached text, but whole chapters, as they had long been committed to its safe, but hitherto unprofitable keeping. The veil was removed from my heart; and Jesus Christ, as the Alpha and Omega, the sum and substance of every thing, shone out upon me just as He is set forth in the everlasting

Gospel. It was the same as if I had been reading, because I knew it so well by rote, only much more rapid, as thought always is. In this there was nothing uncommon; but in the *opening of the understanding, that I might* UNDERSTAND *the Scriptures*, was the mighty miracle of grace and truth. There I lay, still as death, my hands still folded over my eyes, my very soul basking in the pure, calm, holy light that streamed into it through the appointed channel of God's word. Rapture was not what I felt; excitement, enthusiasm, agitation, there was none. I was like a person long enclosed in a dark dungeon, the walls of which had now fallen down, and I looked round on a sunny landscape of calm and glorious beauty. I well remember that the Lord Jesus, in the character of a shepherd, of a star, and, above all, as the pearl of great price, seemed revealed to me most beautifully; that he could save every body, I at once saw; that he would save me, never even took the form of a question. Those who have received the Gospel by man's preaching may doubt and cavil: I took it simply from the Bible, in the words that God's wisdom teacheth, and thus I argued:—"Jesus Christ came into the world to save sinners: I am a sinner: I want to be saved: he will save me." There is no presumption in taking God at his word: not to do so is very impertinent: I did it and I was happy.

After some time I rose from the sofa, and walked about: my feelings were delicious. I had found Him of whom Moses, in the law, and the prophets, did write: I had found the very Paschal Lamb, whose blood would be my safeguard from the destroying angel. Oh, how delicious was that particular thought to me! It was one of the first that occurred, and I laughed with gladness. Indeed my feeling was very joyous, and I only wanted somebody to tell it to. I had two servants, one a young woman, the other a little girl, both papists, both loving me with Irish warmth. They were delighted to see me so well and happy on a sudden, and in the evening I bade them come to my room, for I was going to read a beautiful book, and would read it aloud. I began the gospel of St. Matthew, and read nine chapters to them, their wonder and delight increasing my joy.

Whenever I proposed leaving off, they begged for more; and only for my poor throat I think we should have gone on till day. I prayed with them, and what a night's rest I had! Sleep so sweet, a waking so happy, and a joy so unclouded through the day, what but the gospel could bestow? Few, very few have been so privileged as I was, to be left alone with the infallible teaching of God the Holy Ghost, by means of the written word, for many weeks, and so to get a thorough knowledge of the great doctrines of salvation, unclouded by man's vain wisdom. I knew not that in the world there were any who had made the same discovery with myself. Of all schemes of doctrine I was wholly ignorant, and the only system of theology open to me was God's own. All the faculties of my mind were roused and brightened for the work. I prayed, without ceasing, for divine instruction: and took, without cavilling, what was vouchsafed. On this subject I must enter more largely, for it is one of immense importance.

LETTER VI.

RELIGIOUS PROGRESS.

I am standing before you now in the character of one who, having been brought, under conviction of sin, in utter self-despair, had found in Christ Jesus a refuge from the storm of God's anger. I felt myself safe in Him; but as the revelation which God had made to man was not confined to the alone point of a satisfaction for the sins of men, I felt it my bounden duty to search for all that the Most High had seen good to acquaint his people with. At the same time I found myself a member of a church, calling itself Christian; but I, too, had called myself a Christian, while as yet wholly ignorant of Christ, therefore I could not depend upon a name. I knew there were other churches, each putting in a claim to a higher and purer standard than its neighbours, and it behoved me to know which of them all was in the right. I had no books of a religious character; not one: no clergyman among my acquaintance, no means of inquiry, save as regarded my own church, whose Liturgy and Articles lay before me. I resolved to bring them first to the test of scripture; and if they failed, to look out for a better.

How I commenced the work, and pursued it, I need not state. I tried everything, as well as I could, by the Bible: and my satisfaction was great to find the purest, clearest strain of evangelical truth breathing through the book which I had used all my life long, as I did the Bible, without entering into its real meaning. How I could possibly escape seeing the doctrines of faith, regeneration, and the rest of God's revelation in them both was strange to me; but I understood that the natural man receiveth not the things of the Spirit of God, and mourned over the darkness that I supposed universal.

I found it distinctly stated by our Lord, that "except a man be born again, he cannot see the kingdom of God!" and this served as a key to many passages in the Epistles, and other parts of Scripture illustrative of the same solemn truth. I had never understood, never thought of this. Did my Church hold it? Yes; it was not only laid down as a fundamental doctrine in her Articles but constantly put into the mouths of her congregation, either expressed or clearly implied. Again, I found that not by works but by faith I was to be justified before God; and this also ran through the prayer-book, with unvarying distinctness—though with that book in my hand, and its contents on my lips, I had been, hitherto, attempting to scale heaven by a ladder of my own forming. I then tried the creeds by Scripture, which would have been a very laborious work, unassisted as I was by any exposition or references, had not my memory been well stored with the word of God, while, as I humbly hope, the Holy Spirit took of the things of Christ, and showed them unto me. The only clause in the creeds that startled me was that of our Lord's descent into hell; that he ever visited the place of condemned spirits I could not believe nor do I now believe it, nor ever for a moment since that period gave credit to the monstrous assertion. If by hell is meant the place of separated souls, as I was afterwards told, why not call it by a less ambiguous name? However, I would not for one uncertain phrase, which I then suspected, and now know to be a modern interpolation, reject a whole system. I contented myself with refraining from making that confession; and on all occasions substituting when I could the beautiful Nicene Creed for the other. Of course this declaration will bring on me a storm of censure from some quarters: so be it. I am relating facts; and happy would it be for the church and country, if all who in some minor matters hesitate at using expressions made choice of by the fallible compilers of mere human compositions, would allow themselves the same liberty, instead of falling into schism and swelling the ranks of dissent.

The Athanasian Creed brought to my recollection a circumstance that had occurred a few years before, the importance of which had never been known to me until I was made acquainted with the saving truths of the Gospel. I now looked back upon it with trembling joy, and gratitude to him who had preserved me from a snare into which the pride of intellect, joined to spiritual ignorance, would have been sure to lead me, but for the watchful care of my heavenly Father, still working by means of my blind but sincere reverence for His word. I have mentioned that in my native town Socinianism flourished to a fearful extent; it had long been a very hotbed of that fatal heresy; the holders of which are found among many of those possessing wealth, influence, and high attainments. I knew no more of it than that it was one of the many forms of dissent with which I had nothing to do; I was acquainted with several of its disciples: but as religion formed no part of our social intercourse, its peculiarities were wholly unknown to me.

Not long before my trip to America, I had been staying in Norwich, in the same house with a most clever, intelligent, and amiable woman, of whom I was very fond. I knew her to be a Dissenter, and that was all. One evening she drew me into a conversation, the commencement of which I forget, but it soon arrived at a denial, on her part, of the Godhead of Christ: which exceedingly astonished me, for I never supposed that could be called in question. I ran for the Bible, saying, I would soon shew her that it was not to be disputed; and she in return asserted that I could not prove it out of the *inspired Scriptures.* After pondering for a while, I recollected the first chapter of Revelation, which for its sublimity I ranked amongst the highest of my poetical gems, and that it unequivocally proclaimed the divinity of our glorious Lord. I opened at it, on which she burst into a laugh, saying "You are not so weak as to fancy that book of riddles any part of God's word?" "Why, it is in the Bible, you see," replied I, half indignantly.

"And who put it there? Come, you are a person of too much sense to believe that the binding up of certain leaves between the covers of the Bible makes them a part of it. You must exercise the reason that God has given you: and in so doing you will discover so many interpolations and deceptions in that version of yours, that you will be glad to find a more accurate one."

She continued in the same strain for some time. I was greatly agitated; I closed the great Bible, and leaning on it, with folded arms, my heart beating violently against the bright red cover, I gave heed to all she said. My love of novelty, passion for investigation, and the metaphysical turn that had sometimes made my father quite uneasy about me when he saw me at eight years old poring over abstruse reasonings with the zest of an old philosopher, were all in her favour. I felt as if the foundation of my faith was giving way, and I was being launched on a sea of strange uncertainty. When she concluded, I laid my forehead on the book, in most deep and anxious thought. I did not pray: God was found of one who sought him not; for surely he alone dictated my answer. I started up, and with the greatest vivacity said, "Mrs. ——, If you can persuade me that the book of Revelation is not inspired, another person may do the same with regard to the book of Genesis; and so of all that lie between them, till the whole Bible is taken away from me. That will never do: I cannot part with my dear Bible. I believe it all, every word of it; and I am sure I should be miserable if I did not." Then, kissing the precious volume with the affection one feels for what is in danger of being lost to us, I carried it back to its shelf, and declined any further discussion on the subject. She told some one else she was sure of having me yet: but the good providence of God interposed to remove me from the scene of danger.

That metaphysical turn, I omitted to mention among my early snares: my father checked it, although it was a great hobby of his own. He had seen its fearful abuse in the origin of the French revolution, and regarded it as one of the evil spirits of the age. I recollect the mixture of mirth and vexation depicted in his face one morning, when on remarking that I did not look well, and inquiring if anything ailed me, I replied, "No, but I could not get any sleep."

"What prevented your sleeping?"

"I was thinking, Papa, of '*Cogito, ergo sum*,' and I lay awake, trying to find out all about it."

"'*Cogito, ergo sum!*'" repeated my father, laughing and frowning at the same time, "what will you be at twenty, if you dabble in metaphysics before you are ten? Come, I must set you to study Euclid; that will sober your wild head a little." I took the book with great glee, delighted to have a new field of enquiry; but soon threw it aside. Mathematics and I could never agree. Speculative and imaginative in an extraordinary degree, carrying much sail with scarcely any ballast, what but the ever-watchful care of Him who sitteth upon the circle of the earth could have preserved from fatal wrecking, a vessel so frail, while yet without pilot, helm, or chart!

It was the recollection of my short encounter with the Socinian that satisfied me respecting the Athanasian creed. I felt, that had I taken up its bold assertions and established every one of them, as I now did, by Scripture, no sophistry could have staggered my faith, though it had been but a reasoning, not a saving faith, in that high doctrine of the co-existent, co-equal Trinity. I did not then know—for of all Church history I was ignorant,—that its original object was not so much to establish a truth, as to detect and defeat a falsehood. The damnatory clauses, as they are called, did not startle me. I saw clearly the fact that God had made a revelation of Himself to man, which revelation man was not at liberty to receive or to reject; and as without faith it is impossible to please God, and that alone is faith which implicitly believes the record that he hath given of his Son, the deductions in question were perfectly fair and orthodox. I frequently wondered, when subsequently brought into the arena of various controversies, at the ease with which aided by the Bible alone, I settled so many disputed points; and as it really was by the Bible I settled them, man's teaching has never yet on any subject altered my views.

The only serious difficulty that I met, was in trying to receive the doctrine of election. I read the seventeenth article, where I, at least, found it most palpably insisted on; and I remembered having in childhood, heard many hot disputes on that subject. My grandmother held it, but she was nearly alone in her opinion; and I was accustomed to hear it very much denounced, which no doubt left a prejudice on my mind. I resolved to search it out most diligently; but wishing first to be thoroughly grounded in the vital points of the co-equality of the three persons in the Godhead, I read the book of the Acts with an express view to the latter. In so doing, I became fully and undesignedly convinced on that of election, as held by those called Calvinistic divines, not one of whom to my knowledge, had I ever met with. After this, I traced it in every part of the Scriptures, running like a golden thread through the whole Bible. I have been closely pressed by its opponents on more than one occasion, and urged to read treatises on the subject; but pro or con, no treatises have I read; man can tell me no more than that God has clearly revealed it, therefore man cannot strengthen a belief founded on the sure word of God; or if he tells me it is not revealed, I know that it is; because I have found it so, and relinquish it I never can.

Whether it be regarded as presumptuous, or not, I must thankfully avow that during the weeks when I was left alone with my Bible, I obtained a view of the whole scheme of redemption, and God's dealings with man, which to this hour I have never found reason to alter in any one respect, save as greater light has continually broken in on each branch of the subject, strengthening, not changing those views. You will see in the progress of my sketch, how complete a bulwark against error in numberless shapes I have found in this simple adherence to the plain word of truth: this habit of bringing every proposition "to the law and to the testimony;" fully persuaded that "if they speak not according to this word, it is because there is no light in them."

I now proceed to an interesting epoch in my life: the commencement of my literary labours in the Lord's cause. It marks very strongly the over-ruling hand of Him who was working all things after the counsel of his own will; and I will give it you without curtailment, together with my introduction, through it, to the Christian community of the land.

My life, as I told you, was solitary and retired; my time chiefly passed in writing out documentary matters for the lawyers. The law-suit, concerning a property not worth litigating, had already been carried into three courts, Chancery, King's Bench, and Prerogative, and the labour devolving on me was most irksome. The circumstance of my using the pen so incessantly became known, and I was looked on as a literary recluse. One day a lady, personally unknown to me, but whose indefatigable zeal was always seeking the good of others, sent me a parcel of tracts. With equal wonder and delight I opened one of them, a simple, spiritual little production; and the next that I took up was an inducement to distribute tracts among the poor. From this I learned that some excellent people were engaged in a work quite new to me; and, with a sigh, I wished I had the means of contributing to their funds. Presently the thought flashed upon me, "Since I cannot give them money, may I not write something to be useful in the same way?" I had just then no work before me; and a long winter evening at command. I ordered large candles, told the servants not to interrupt me, and sat down to my novel task. I began about seven o'clock, and wrote till three in the morning; when I found I had produced a complete little story, in the progress of which I had been so enabled to set forth the truth as it is in Jesus, that on reading it over I was amazed at the statement I had made of scriptural doctrine, and sunk on my knees in thankfulness to God. Next morning, I awoke full of joy, but much puzzled, as to what I should do with my tract. At length, in the simplicity of my heart, I resolved to send it to the Bishop of Norwich, and busied myself, at the breakfast-table, in computing how many franks it would fill. While thus employed, a note was put into my hands, from Miss D., apologizing for the liberty taken; saying, she had sent me, the day before, some tracts, and as she heard I was much occupied with the pen, it had occurred to her that I might be led to write something myself, in the possibility of which she now enclosed the address of the Secretary to the Dublin Tract Society, to whom such aid would be most welcome.

I was absolutely awe-struck by this very marked incident. I saw in it a gracious acceptance of my free-will offering at His hands to whom it had been prayerfully dedicated; and in two hours the manuscript was on its way to Dublin, with a very simple letter to the Secretary. A cordial answer, commendatory of my tract, and earnestly entreating a continuance of such aid, soon reached me, with some remarks and questions that required a fuller communication of my circumstances and feelings. He had recommended frequent intercourse with the peasantry, of whose habits and modes of expression I was evidently ignorant, and I then mentioned my loss of hearing as a bar to that branch of usefulness. His rejoinder was the overflowing of a truly Christian heart, very much touched by the artless account of the Lord's dealings with me; and greatly did my spirit rejoice at having found a brother in the faith thus to cheer and strengthen me.

But alas! a few days afterwards, Miss D. whom I had still never seen, wrote to apprize me that this excellent man had ruptured a blood-vessel and was dying. Still he did not forget me, but after lingering for some weeks on his death-bed, commended me to the friendship of his brother, who from that period proved a true and valuable helper to me.

Meanwhile I was beginning to take a view of Popery under the light of the Gospel. As yet, I knew nothing of it spiritually, and my retired life kept me from observing how it worked among the poor people around. My attention was first directed to it by a conversation with the younger of my two servants; she slept in my apartment, and I remarked that while kneeling at her devotions she not only uttered them with amazing rapidity, but carried on all the while the operation of undressing, with perfect inattention to what she was saying. I asked her the purport of her prayers; she told me she said the "Our Father," and then the "Hail Mary:" at my request she repeated the latter, and I gave her a gentle lecture on the irreverence of chattering to God so volubly, and of employing herself about her clothes at the same time; adding that she should be devout, deliberate, and quiet while speaking to God, but as for the Virgin Mary it was no matter how she addressed her, if address her she would, for being only a dead woman she could know nothing about it. This, I am ashamed to say, was the extent of my actual protest at the time. The girl took it all very readily, and ever after, during her address to God she knelt with her hands joined, repeating the words slowly and seriously; but the moment she commenced the "Hail Mary," to make up for lost time she prattled it so rapidly, and tore open the fastenings of her dress with such bustling speed, that I could scarcely refrain from laughing. A little reflection, however, convinced me it was an act of idolatry, and no laughing matter; and from that time I enquired as deeply as I could into their faith and practice; constantly showing them from the Scriptures how contrary their religion was to that of the gospel. Still it was but a very partial and superficial view that I could as yet obtain of the great mystery of iniquity through these ignorant and thoughtless girls; and to this must be attributed my sad failure in not warning them more distinctly to come out of Babylon. I rather tried to patch up the old, decayed, tattered garment with the new piece of the gospel, as many more have done; and so to make the rent worse, instead of replacing the vile article with one of God's providing.

One of the most interesting and delightful subjects opened to me by my study of the Scriptures during this happy period was that of the Jews. I had always felt deeply interested for them, and looked forward to their conversion, individually, to Christ; but nationally I was still in the dark about them. Now, I plainly saw the nature and extent of God's covenanted pledge to Abraham, and became fully convinced that their future national restoration was a revealed truth, and that the church would never attain to any triumph on earth in which the Jews, as Jews, did not bear a very prominent part.

Happily untaught in the spiritualizing process by which the Divine promises to Israel are wrested from their evident, literal sense, I took all that I read as primarily applicable to those who were distinctly addressed by name, though plainly seeing that there was an allowable adaptation of them to the Gentile church. Many a time have I knelt down with the ninth chapter of Daniel spread before me, fervently and with tears pleading in his words for his people. It was not until long afterwards that on urging upon a pious clergyman the duty of combining in some great effort for the conversion of the Jews, I learnt to my surprise and delight of the existence of such a society. I need not tell you that the impression made on my mind by the Bible, when I had no other teacher, has been continually deepening for twenty years; and that nothing which man could say or write ever for a moment shook my conviction on the subject. I laid hold on the word of promise, and urged it on all within my reach from my very first intercourse with Christians; and I have watched with joy the rapid unfolding of God's purposes towards the Jews, both in disposing the hearts of Gentiles towards their cause, and in evidently preparing the way for their speedy restoration.

When that excellent man, Mr. D. was committed to the grave, his younger brother visited me on his way back to Dublin. That interview I shall never forget; he talked to me out of the overflowings of a heart devoted to Christ, and left me pining for more extended enjoyment of Christian society. I was not long ungratified; within three days an unexpected summons took me to Dublin, and on the very evening of my arrival Mr. D. introduced me to a party of about thirty pious friends, assembled to meet a missionary just returned from Russia. Remember, these were the frank, unrestrained, warm-hearted Irish, of all people the most ready at expressing their zealous and generous feelings; and imagine if you can my enjoyment, after such a long season of comparative loneliness, when they came about me with the affectionate welcome that none can utter and look so eloquently as they can! I thought it a foretaste of the heavenly blessedness; and yet I often longed for those seasons when I had none but my God to commune with, and poured out to Him all that now I found it delightful to utter to my fellow-creatures. Then, my tabernacle was indeed pitched in the wilderness, and the candle of the Lord shone brightly upon it; now, the blending of many inferior lights distracted my mind from its one object of contemplation, and broke the harmony that was so sweet in its singleness.

A few months after this, the law-suit being ended, my husband was ordered abroad. I declined to cross the Atlantic a second time, and from this period I became chiefly dependent on my own exertions. My mother had joined me in Ireland, having been made a partaker in the like precious faith and hope with myself. The next event to which I shall advert is a strong temptation to separate from the established church, under circumstances that have led very many to forsake the pale of her communion. I have observed that, at the time in question, there was no gospel preached in the pulpits of the establishment near me; I, however, a year after my reception of the truth, became acquainted with a most godly, zealous, and truly able minister who officiated in the Independent chapel. We found that he had to travel late at night or to put up at an inn, as his regular charge was at some distance, and we freely offered him such hospitality as our house would afford. He took no unfair advantage to urge us into his own communion; but the contrast of his character and deportment to those of the pleasure-loving divines to whom we had been long accustomed; the spirituality of his conversation, the excellency of his preaching, and the privilege of his domestic ministry in our little household at his weekly visit, all wrought to predispose me when, in the way of equal communication, we came to discuss the grounds of his dissent. Had I not already brought my prayer-book to the test, in the way related, before any bias could disturb my mind, I really think I should have been overcome in an argument where the odds were so strong against me; but thus prepared I could repel all charges on fundamental points; and in matters indifferent I refused to recognize a sufficient excuse for separating from what in its constitution was decidedly scriptural and good. My church was taxed with being essentially popish, and in rebutting this I became better acquainted with her essential protestantism. She was denounced as a worldly secular system, opposed to the declaration of our Lord, that his kingdom is not of this world; but I had sense enough to see and to point out the total irrelevancy of that hackneyed quotation to the subject of ecclesiastical establishments. The unholy lives of too many of her clergy, with their shameful neglect of the souls committed to them, I could not deny; but already a great revival had taken place among the Irish parochial clergy; it was proceeding rapidly; and while this evidenced that God was still with her, I could also point to the ordination vows, and show that it was to the wickedness of individuals in breaking the most solemn engagements, not to any defect in the system, or any lack of strong injunctions to zeal, diligence, and devotion, we must attribute the acknowledged evils existing among others. My friend too, always mild, kind, and charitable on other subjects, generally laid aside these characteristics when on this, and assailed the established Church with the weapons of ridicule, sarcasm, scorn, and bitterness, which certainly produced on me the contrary effect to what was intended. He seemed to me to pay little attention to the spiritual wants of the poor deluded Romanists; rather seeking to convert episcopalians into dissenters, than papists into Christians. Measuring all things by the standard of the written word, I became more fully convinced the more I examined the matter, that there was no just cause why a believer should quit the communion of a church clearly built on the foundation of the prophets and apostles; and even under the disadvantages of such a location as I have described, I continued firm in my attachment to her. Some people told me I ought to take higher ground in upholding the episcopal establishment of this country: if they will point out to me any ground higher than the top of the rock whereon I believe her to stand, that rock being Christ, I will take it; but none, none so high, none so sure can be found. Apostolical succession in office is a good thing when the succession in doctrine is equally clear; otherwise they who now officiate in the mosque of Omar, standing on the site of the temple in Jerusalem, and he who sits supreme in the see of Rome, the man of sin, and son of perdition, may respectively claim succession to the Aaronic priesthood and the apostolic ministry. I do not deny that a regular succession exists in the British churches, derived from an apostolic mission, long before Augustine or any other Romish emissary set foot on our soil to pollute the stream; but I should never for a moment dream of adducing that as an argument against one who calls in question the scripturality of our church; since in so doing I might admit the Mother of harlots and abominations of the earth to a participation in the privileges which none but the Lamb's pure wife has any claim to. For my own part I had never heard of such a thing, when God enabled me to stand firm as a member of this maligned church of England; and it is one of the many cases in which I had nothing to unlearn, just because man had taught me nothing, but all I knew was drawn from the clear fountain of eternal truth, opened in the pages of that precious volume, for the gift of which all praise and glory be to God, through Christ Jesus, now and for ever!

LETTER VII.

KILKENNY.

I am now to bring you into the stirring scenes of that time and place where the rebellious spirit of popish agitation had just broken out afresh in Ireland. An invitation to pass some weeks in the county Kilkenny led us to it as guests; and inducements which it was not easy to resist fixed us there as residents for three years. In this part of my narrative no disguise is needful; the facts are before the world, and the estimable man who was made the first victim of this atrocious conspiracy is gone to his rest, after patiently enduring years of persecution, of exile, and of bodily and mental suffering, induced by the scenes he was compelled to pass through.

Vicarsfield, the beautiful parsonage of Dr. Hamilton, is in the county, ten Irish miles from the town, of Kilkenny. Knocktopher is the parish; and at that time the old church was standing, about half a mile from the vicarage, which stood secluded, withdrawn from the public road, nestled in the rich foliage of many fine trees, and adorned with lovely pleasure-grounds. It was the happy privilege of that truly pious minister to originate the clerical meetings which were so eminently, so extensively blessed to the clergy of that diocese, over which his father had presided as bishop. For many years they were held at his house, and truly rich were these seasons to all who inhabited it! Dr Hamilton was a man of fine mind, deep erudition, unbounded benevolence, and Christian sweetness that endeared him to every one. His income was considerable; and while exercising the rites of a truly Irish hospitality on a noble scale, he expended a large proportion of that income in the works of charity, equally judicious, liberal, and impartial. He had under his roof thirteen poor girls, who were educated, maintained, taught in all the requisites of good household servants, and finally placed out in the families of his friends. Mrs Hamilton seemed to have her heart in this school, over which a very competent mistress presided, and a more beautifully-ordered little nursery of valuable domestics I never saw. Besides this, large benefactions were distributed, in clothing, fuel, and other necessaries, among the poor of the parish, without any regard to religious distinction; and as the Romanists amounted to about twelve hundred, while the Protestants could not muster one hundred, and the former were infinitely more necessitous than the latter, of course nearly all went to them. I dwell upon these things, and upon the exceeding kind-heartedness of the good clergyman and his affectionate partner towards their poor neighbours, because it throws additional light on the real origin of those acts which the English people were made to believe resulted from oppression on the part of the Protestant clergy.

When first I went to Knocktopher in the summer of 1821, no open act of violence had been committed or publicly threatened, in its immediate vicinity; but already the name of Captain Rock was becoming formidable. The place borders on Tipperary, from whence came nocturnal parties, scouring the country and alarming the inhabitants on a small scale, while the prelude to much darker scenes was to be traced in the wide circulation of what were called the prophecies of Pastorini. A Dr. Walmsley, a Popish priest, had written a commentary on the book of Revelation, under that name; wherein he explained the ascent of the locusts out of the bottomless pit to prefigure the rise of Protestantism with Luther at its head; calculating the date of their continuance from 1525, and fixing its termination in 1825. Extracts from this impudently mischievous work were disseminated in every possible form among the Romanists; they were translated into

Irish, sent in large numbers to every district to be circulated by careful agents: published in handbills, exhibited in placards, and sung in doggrel rhyme through the streets. There was no article of their faith more devoutly believed by the besotted people, than that in 1825 the Protestants of Ireland and of every other country were, by divine appointment, to be put to death, except such as should recant; and while the lower orders prepared with terrible alacrity to execute the will of God by a general massacre of their unoffending neighbours, those of higher rank and gentler spirits applied themselves to the work of converting their Protestant friends.

Tokens of the rising storm were visible to those who watched for them; the peasantry began to exchange their courteous, respectful demeanour towards the Protestant gentry for a bearing that bespoke either defiance or lurking malignity. Threatening notices poured in upon the landlords who presumed to dispose of their property as they chose; and upon the clergy who, in default of payment, were obliged to serve processes for the tithe. Proctors were way-laid, process-servers cruelly murdered, and the organizations of hostile bodies became daily more apparent. As yet, however, we dwelt in comparative security; Dr. Hamilton often rode out with me to the very verge of the dreadful Tipperary; and his lady drove my mother in her little phaeton to the boundaries of Waterford. No unusual precautions were taken in the way of bolts and bars; and when the good Doctor calmly put into his pocket some of the many letters delivered at the breakfast-table, after a slight glance at their contents, none of us suspected that they were Rockite notices, fiercely threatening his life and signed in blood. He applied privately for a body of police, who were stationed at an old mansion, midway between Vicarsfield and the Tipperary pass, called Castle Morris; and when committing his household to the Lord's keeping, at our evening worship, the deep earnestness of his manner, the resigned look and slight tremor of his frame awoke no suspicions in us. We saw him "sorrowful, yet always rejoicing;" and attributed to the pressure of that bodily indisposition under which he generally laboured, what was indeed referable to the solicitude of a mind that preferred to bear its burden alone rather than hasten the time of our painful participation in the terrors that flesh must needs feel.

At the end of our prolonged visit, we were led to take up our abode in the town of Kilkenny, so richly blessed with gospel privileges, and so far removed from the annoyances to which I was exposed while trying to fulfil the landlord's part over a property inextricably involved, and now also placed in the hands of trustees. I had sought the maintenance of that character for the sake of the poor tenants, whose affection for me was very great, and among whom I had of late been frequently allowed to read the Scriptures. The necessity, however, of providing for myself, and the hopeless perplexities of my nominal office, between head-landlords, under-tenants, trustees, a receiver, and all the endless machinery of an embarrassed little Irish estate, compelled me to seek a more quiet sphere, and in Kilkenny I found all that could combine to encourage me in the pursuit of honest independence, in the way of usefulness. I finished "Osric," which formed a good-sized volume, and commenced the pleasant task of writing penny and twopenny books for the Dublin Tract Society, who paid me liberally, and cheered me on my path with all the warmth of Christian affection. It was indeed a delightful task, and God had raised up to me also a friend to whose truly paternal kindness I owe more than can ever be told;—Mr. George Sandford, now Lord Mountsandford, who from our first acquaintance, entered with a father's interest into all that concerned me. Thus encouraged, I held on my way, and tasted the sweets that I hoped to enjoy to the end of my days—those of the original curse brightened by the irreversible blessing. "In the sweat of thy face shalt thou eat bread"—"Be ye stedfast, unmoveable, always abounding in the work of the Lord, forasmuch as ye know that your labour shall not be in vain in the Lord."

I have already told you of my escape from the snare of Socinianism. I have noticed the grounds on which I declined to separate from the Established Church; and now I am to narrate a trial of faith and doctrine, which by the mercy of God produced effects just the reverse of what was intended. This was no less than a vigorous attempt to convert me to Popery! I had not yet bestowed any great attention on the details of that abominable device, but was most fully persuaded of its being a system of idolatrous delusion, the working of which was strikingly manifested in the wretchedness, the immorality, the turbulence and degrading superstitions of the poor creatures around me. It never had been my practice to tamper or compromise with what I knew to be wrong; hence I had not suffered curiosity to lead me within the walls of a mass-house, nor in any way to put on the semblance of an agreement which cannot really exist between the temple of God and idols. I believed Popery to be the Babylon of the Apocalypse, and I longed for resolution to proclaim to the deluded victims, "Come out of her, my people!" This I had never done, but on the contrary fell cheerfully in with the then cautious policy of my friends, and so framed my little books and tracts as to leave it doubtful whether they were written by a Protestant or not. Paul to the Jews became as a Jew that he might gain the Jews: I, by a false process of reason, thought it allowable to become as an idolator to the idolators that I might gain the idolators. An awfully presumptuous sin! The Jew possesses the fair blossom of Gospel truth, which by kindly fostering is to be expanded and ripened into the rich fruit: the Papist holds in his hand an apple of Sodom, beneath the painted rind of which is a mass of ashes and corruption. He must be induced to fling it away, and to pluck from the tree of life a wholly different thing.

My Protestant principles, such as they were, withheld me from visiting the convent, which formed a principal attraction to the military, and other strangers in Kilkenny. Many sought to draw me thither, adducing the examples of Christian ministers and other spiritual people, who did not scruple to go; but in vain. At length a lady came to me with an earnest request from "the most interesting nun in the establishment" to give her some information on the best mode of conveying instruction to a poor little girl in their school, deaf and dumb. Here was a call of duty: I knew it could not be effectually done unless in person; and to the surprise of my friend I volunteered to accompany her to the convent.

The nun was indeed a most engaging young lady: in personal appearance, in manner, in feeling, realizing the visions of my girlish romance when reading idle stories in novels on such topics. She had, moreover, all the animated warmth of a genuine Irishwoman, and her fine countenance, beaming with benevolent joy at our successful beginning, and with affectionate gratitude for my services, quite won my heart. I promised to repeat the visit shortly, and on doing so accompanied her to walk round the garden, at the other extremity of which stood a building which I took for their school, and unhesitatingly mounted the stairs with my sweet conductor. Judge what was my dismay when, on passing the folding-doors, I found myself in a splendid Popish chapel, opposite the altar, over which shone a richly gilt cross, while my poor nun was prostrated in the lowliest adoration, touching the ground with her forehead before the senseless idol!

I was confounded, and unable to say anything; but after a hasty glance at the fine trappings, left the place, secretly praying for grace and strength to protest openly against the abomination, from which my soul revolted with unspeakable horror from the moment of my witnessing the act of idolatrous homage rendered to a thing of wood and stone. On leaving the convent, I met a person who informed me that my poor nun was a Protestant lady of high respectability, sprung from one of those iniquitous mixed marriages, her mother belonging to the Established Church, her father a Romanist, who however, honestly adhered to the terms of the wicked covenant by which the sons were to be educated in his, the latter in her persuasion. A family of daughters were born to them, who with their mother continued nominally Protestant; but after his death, when the house was filled with Romish priests, performing for a week together their mummeries over the corpse, these poor females had become a prey to the subtle perversions of the ecclesiastics, and had openly apostatized— save my new friend, who with a better-informed mind and more scriptural knowledge withstood their sophistries, until sundry mock miracles performed by means of saintly relics, and a well-contrived nocturnal visitation from the ghost of her father, whom she fondly loved, had so unnerved and frightened her that she too fell a prey to the delusion. They ended by admitting her into the sisterhood of this convent, excusing the payment of the large sum usually demanded; and as her darkness was now great in proportion to the measure of light against which she had sinned, they found her a valuable decoy-bird to draw others into the snare. I did not learn all these particulars at the time, nor until after her decease, when I met with a near family connection of hers who told them to me: I simply gleaned the fact of her apostacy, with that of her abounding zeal in the antichristian cause.

With all my heart I loved the gentle, affectionate, elegant nun, and earnestly did I pray for help in bringing her back, as I was resolved to do, from the path of destruction; and while I deliberated on the best means of commencing the work, the difficulty was removed by her openly attempting to convert me. To this end she urged on me a strict enquiry into the real doctrines and tenets of her church, for myself and by myself, promising to lend me books of the most candid character if I would engage to read them. I agreed, stipulating that I was freely to write out my remarks on them, for her consideration; and with this mutual understanding I brought home from the convent the precious loan of Dr. Milner's "End of Controversy," furnished for my especial benefit by a seminary of Jesuit Priests, located near the town: and thus was I become the object of a combined attack from the forces of Great Babylon.

True to what I considered a tacit engagement to study the matter alone, I read the book. Never shall I forget the effect it produced on me. I seemed to be holding communion with Satan himself, robed as an angel of light, the transparent dra- pery revealing his hideous form, but baffling my endeavours to rend it away. Such sophistry, such impudence of unsupported assertion, such distortion of truth, and gilding of gross falsehood, I never met with. I tried in vain to find an answer to things that I saw and felt to be anti-scriptural and destructive: but this "End" was the beginning of my controversy, for I was wholly new to it, and ignorant of the historical and other facts necessary to disprove the reverend author's bold assumptions. At last I burst into tears, and kneeling down, exclaimed, "O Lord, I cannot unravel this web of iniquity: enable me to cut it in twain!" I was answered; for after a little more thought, a broad view of the whole scheme of man's salvation as revealed in the Holy Scriptures appeared to me the best antidote for this insidious poison. I read through the New Testament with increased enjoyment, and casting from me the wretched fabric of lies, with all its flimsy pretences, I resolved instead of attempting a reply to what I saw to be falsehood, to set forth a plain statement of what I knew to be truth. Indeed it is indescribable how disgusting the painted face, the gaudy trappings, and the arrogant assumptions of the Great Harlot appeared in my eyes, when thus contrasted with the sublime simplicity, purity, and modesty of the chaste Spouse of Christ.

I wrote; and in reply got another and a smaller book, containing the pretended reasons of a Protestant for embracing Popery. They were, of course, artfully put, and made a formidable exhibition of the peril of heresy. I thought I could not do better in return, while writing my dissent, to enclose some small books of my own to the nun, inviting her comments thereon. This brought a letter which was probably written by stealth, though so cautiously worded as to be safe if intercepted. She said she did not wish to leave me under a wrong impression, and therefore told me that she was not permitted to read any of my letters, or the little books I had sent; as those who watched over her spiritual interests, and whom she was bound to obey, thought it wrong to unsettle her mind by reading any thing contrary to the true faith which she held. Here was a pretty exposure of one-sided honesty! I thanked God for the further insight given me into the Mystery of Iniquity, and from that day devoted all my powers to the investigation of that against which I had become a staunch Protester.

In the midst of our proceedings, a nun had taken the veil at the convent. Every body almost, to their shame be it spoken, was trying for tickets to see the unhallowed show. My poor friend sent us two, informed me that two of the best front seats would be reserved for us, and accompanied her kind note with a programme of the ceremony, and a translation or transcription of the service, all in her own handwriting. I felt deeply the pain of hurting her, and perhaps also for a moment the workings of natural curiosity, but the hesitation was short; I sent back both books and tickets, with a grateful but decided refusal to be present. In all Kilkenny I did not find a person who could go along with me in my objections; but it is a matter of great joy to me to this hour that I kept myself wholly unpolluted by any participation in these idolatrous doings; and I do believe that a double blessing has attended my efforts against Popery in consequence of it.

Before I take you on a second and very different visit to Vicarsfield, I will anticipate a little, and tell you of a subsequent attack made on my faith from a quarter far unlike the former. The affair of the little deaf mute at the convent led me to turn my attention to some poor children similarly circumstanced in the streets of Kilkenny; and while prosecuting that work, the Lord brought to me that dear dumb boy, whom you well remember as the brightest, most lovely of Christian characters. He was then very little, and had a brother of sixteen, one of the most genuine Paddies I ever beheld. This lad was living very idly; a fine sensible shrewd fellow who could read and write, and very soon made a great proficiency in the finger language by helping me to instruct Jack. No one above Pat's own rank had ever taken any interest in him; I did, a strong one; and as he was much with me, and of a character most intensely Irish, he became attached to me with a warmth of devotion rarely met with among any other people.

One day Pat made his appearance with an important look, his brogues stamping the carpet with unwonted energy, his fine bare throat stiffened into a sort of dignified hauteur and his very keen hazle eyes sparkling under the bushy luxuriance of chestnut curls that clustered about his face and fell on his neck. The very beau-ideal of a wild Irish youth was my friend Pat. Seating himself, as usual, he began—and here I must observe that my chief knowledge of the phraseology and turn of thought so peculiar to the Irish peasant was derived from this source. Whenever Pat came "to discourse me" I got rich lessons in the very brogue itself from the fidelity with which his spelling followed the pronunciation of his words.—"I wouldn't like," said he, "that you would go to hell."

"Nor I either, Pat."

"But you are out of the thrue church, and you won't be saved, and I must convart ye."

"That is very kind of you, my good lad: If I am wrong you cannot do better than set me right."

"Sure and I will."

"But how?"

"With this," said he, pulling out a small pamphlet, nothing the cleaner for wear. "You must learn my Catechism, and it's you that will be the good Catholic."

Delighted with the boy's honest zeal, I asked him where I should begin; and he, no less pleased at my docility, desired me to read it all, and then get it all by heart. I promised to do the first at any rate; and oh what a tissue of falsehood and blasphemy that "Butler's Catechism" was! Next morning my teacher came early: "Well, Pat, I have found out what makes you anxious about me; here it is said that none can be saved out of the true Church."

"That's it, sure enough."

"But I do belong to the true Church, and I'll shew you what it is"—so I pointed out to him two passages, and added, "Now I do love our Lord Jesus Christ in sincerity, and therefore I am one of those to whom St. Paul wishes grace and peace; and do you think an apostle would send his blessing to any body who was not of the true Church?"

Pat shook his head: "That's *your* catechism, not mine."

"Very true; Dr Butler wrote yours, and God wrote mine," holding up the Bible; "which is best?"

"That is not the real Bible," persisted Pat, "my priest has the true Bible."

"Then ask him to lend you his."

"I wouldn't get my ears pulled, would I?" said he, smiling: "but if he lent me his Bible he must lend me a car to bring it home in, for it's as big as this table. Your's is too little, and does'nt hold half the truth. That is why you are so ignorant."

I soon proved, by shewing him Matthew Henry's Commentary, that the word of God would lie in a very small compass, the great bulk of the book being man's work. I also urged on him the absolute necessity of reading what God had given for our learning, and the danger of resting on man's assertion. Pat stood his ground most manfully, astonishing me by the adroitness with which he parried my attacks, while pursuing, as he hoped, the good work of my conversion. For many a day was the controversy carried on; Butler *versus* the Bible,—without any other effect than that of bringing Pat to read the sacred book for himself; but it opened to me the awful wiles of darkness by which the poor and ignorant are blinded, while for the more educated class such polished sophistry as Milner's is carefully prepared. I reaped the fruit, however, six years afterwards, when, in a little English church, Pat kneeled beside me and his brother, a thankful communicant at the Lord's table.

Our next visit to Vicarsfield displayed a melancholy change indeed in that sweet spot. There were iron bars, and chains, and double bolts superadded to the hospitable hall-door; the large window in the dining-room, from which we were wont to step out upon a rising lawn, was blocked up by an immense piece of wood, half a foot in thickness, fixed on the inside, to support which a solid beam, pressing against it, was built into the floor of the room with mortar, resting just behind the chair where the lady of the house did the honours of the table; the servants being obliged to stride over it when waiting on her.

Every pannel of every shutter, above and below, had an alarm-bell attached, besides the strongest fastenings that could be contrived. All the plate, save that required for daily use, was taken to Lord Carrick's, who had made his noble mansion, Mount-Juliet, a strong-hold, where were deposited the arms and valuables of his less fortified neighbours. At sun-set, every door was barricaded, every window closed, and no Romanist allowed, on any pretext, to enter the house. The only person of that persuasion attached to the establishment was the gardener, of whose personal fidelity they had no doubt; but his wife was a devotee, and they well knew that every tie of affection and gratitude must give way before the stern despotism of the merciless creed. Some dreadful murders had lately been perpetrated very near; a barrack was burned, and several policemen butchered in a surprize. Dr. Hamilton had been openly and fiercely threatened: his proctor was way-laid, and he narrowly escaped assassination; and to realize more awfully what had otherwise been but matter of report, I was shown from the window of the drawing-room, at noon-day, a body of Rockites, to the number of forty, well mounted, formidably armed, with cross-belts and cartouche-boxes, leisurely walking their horses within less than a quarter of a mile from the house, for the purpose of intimidation. It was close by the *bohreen*, or narrow lane, where, a few years afterwards, the dreadful massacre of Carrickshock took place, which finally drove my persecuted friends from their home and country.

These were the days of *Captain Rock's* terrible rule, of which a record is left in the heart's blood of many an Irishman. A vile book, from the pen of Mr. Moore, under that title, helped forward the work among a rank who were well known to take the lead in this rebellious movement; for although the executioners of decrees pronounced by the invisible tribunal were found to be of a class peculiarly ignorant and lawless, it was not by such hands the main body was organized and its ramifications directed, nor by such hands that the various missives were penned. The work undertaken was to level that great constitutional breakwater which breasted the tumultuous waves as they raged without, affording a smooth haven of security within its boundaries; and the argument used was anything but complimentary to the common sense of those whom it addressed; being, in fact, that the external violence was wholly occasioned by the aforesaid breakwater, not by the natural constitution of the conflicting elements engaged in it,—level the barrier, the waves will subside, and flow evenly to the quiet shore. Wherefore, then, was the rampart-stone placed there? What induced the men of a preceding generation to present such a front to the stormy ocean? Winds and waves, it was again replied, were different in former days from what they now are; the idle prejudice is exploded, that invested nature's laws with unchangeableness, and billows are not now what they were three centuries ago. To urge home this powerful logic, alike to the hopes and fears of man, if it failed to reach their understandings, was the object kept in view by the entire confederacy of Rome, who had at heart the supremacy in Ireland of that system whereof Doyle was the Priest, O'Connell the Politician, and Moore the Poet and Historian. To the work of the two former, due praise on the one hand, due execration on the other, was accorded: to the latter not. The nobleman who boasted that he sang the last of the Stuarts out of three kingdoms with his "Lillebulero" song was forgotten; the demagogue who said to a constitutional opponent, "Do you make the laws of the nation, only let me write their ballads," was forgotten too: while the rhymer of the Propaganda guided the serpent of rebellion to its mark, under the flowery covert of his loose poetry; gaining to himself a name as the laureate of voluptuousness, that should the better mask his object when launching forth in sober prose on the wild sea of politics. I read that pernicious book amid the terrors, the desolations, and afflictions that it was purposely framed to help on; and when closing the insidious volume, I looked forward to the proceedings of a higher and juster tribunal than that which awards so unequal a retribution to him who singly murders with a pike, and him who by whole-sale murders with a pen; that dooms the poor, ignorant, untaught, deluded Peasant to infamy and a halter, while it recompenses the intellectual, refined, deluding Poet with fame and a pension.

LETTER VIII.

THE WORKINGS OF POPERY.

Although, perhaps, too late to be instructive to this generation, it is painfully interesting to look back upon the subtlety and skill that wove a snare for our expediency-loving rulers. Man may meet man in his own strength, moral or physical; but when Satan buckles on his infernal weapons wherewith to assail the individual or national allegiance of those who profess to serve God, nothing but the shield of faith CAN resist him. That shield had been upheld during the life of our believing king: but now he was gone; and right justly did the enemy calculate on the advantages afforded to him by a relaxed and powerless grasp. Like the symbolical Britannia of our coinage, we rested upon the shield, more as a matter of display than of use; and so left the bosom bare to every shaft.

Our enemies know well, though we do not always admit it, that the insuperable barrier to the domination of Popery in these realms, is the Established Church: so long as its ministers hold the pure, high doctrines of uncompromising Protestantism, set forth in all her creeds and formularies. As yet it had not occurred to the invisible head of the Anti-christian confederacy to make good a lodgement within these defences; or rather I ought to say he had not permission so to do, until the Church, represented in the legislature by her chief pastors, and out of it by a number of her officiating ministers, had acquiesced in the abominable act of national apostacy. The church of Ireland was far less guilty in this matter than that of England; among her really spiritual clergy I do not think she numbered three Emancipators; and let it ever be remembered how the beloved Archbishop—the last of Tuam's Archbishops—even to the fatal day of that surrender, lifted a solemn protesting voice against it in the house of Peers. At the time of which I now write, the increasing spirituality of the Irish clergy, bearing its natural fruit in increased love for the souls of men and zeal for Christ's cause, presented an alarming obstacle in the way of those who might fearlessly have advanced through a host of "dumb dogs," sleeping at their posts, as the predecessors of this generation too commonly did. Hitherto they had found only the name and form of a Protestant Church to oppose them; now the living reality started up in their path, and they must remove it ere success could be hoped for. Hence the anti-tithe war; the first alarm of which was openly sounded in the parish, and the first sanguinary onset menaced against the house, wherein I was a guest. What a contemptuous, yet, alas! what a just estimate must the earthly leaders of this civil work have formed of the blind infatuation possessing the rulers of our political destinies! Regarding them as ready-made fools, they proceeded accordingly to take advantage of their folly: and for this we can only account by remembering that the whole movement was directed by one who has had six thousand years' experience in such matters, and who knows that when the kings of earth, from Adam downwards, cast off the bond of obedience to the King of kings, ruin to themselves and to all that appertains to them, will surely follow. He saw that hallowed bond loosening, until a touch might sever it: then he, who believes and trembles, took a devilish advantage of those who believed not and were fearless.

Against the established church a violent outcry was raised, a furious onslaught conducted, by those who avowedly aimed at revolutionizing every thing: *therefore* and *thereby* they whose object it was to avert such revolution were to be convinced that the outpost so fiercely attacked was a hindrance, not in the way of the assailants, but of the defenders of the citadel! Would any human intellect have imagined such an enterprise unaided by

Satan himself in the plenitude of his infernal sagacity? I think not. Yet it did succeed, so far as man was concerned. The means of defence extended to the clergy were wholly inadequate from the beginning of the fray; and as it advanced, those means were by all possible contrivances curtailed and withdrawn. Knocktopher was the known point of the attack, and how was it guarded? A handful of policemen occupied a retired post nearly two miles distant; and when the hostile demonstrations became incessant, and much blood had been shed, a small detachment of military was stationed somewhat nearer. Kilkenny maintained 24,000 most devoted Romanists, with about 800 Protestants, many of them so only in name; the spirit manifested there was most turbulent, and many daring outrages were perpetrated; yet to garrison this important town, and to protect the whole country round, from hosts of armed and disciplined rebels, that invaluable officer Colonel Lindsay had only his gallant Highland regiment, the 78th, on its peace establishment. Little note is now-a-days taken of such services as Colonel Lindsay rendered; but the poor hunted Protestants of that country will not soon forget his wisdom, vigilance, and zeal on their behalf. He disposed his small force with admirable judgment, so far as it could possibly be made to extend; and often did he take his departure from head-quarters, carelessly saying he was going to pass a day or two at Desart, at Mount-Juliet, or other neighbouring seats where he was ever a welcome visitant; when few besides those who met him on his rounds suspected that the gallant soldier passed his nights in the saddle, scouring the perilous country, and keeping watch over those who were marked for destruction. I have no doubt on my mind that Colonel Lindsay was personally, in a very high degree, instrumental in checking the operations of those who, watchful for harm as he was for good, knew his proceedings, and shrank from his protecting eye. I well remember that when Sir Denis Packe was brought for interment to the cathedral of his native Kilkenny, we all supposed the regiment had nearly its full complement of Highlanders in barrack; and Colonel Lindsay confessed to me he was dreadfully at a loss, being unable to turn out above eighty men for an occasion demanding the fullest display he could afford. It required no small measure of military finesse to make us feel that we were protected, and the enemy that he was held in check, over so extensive a ground, while in reality the disposable force was wholly inadequate to do either.

But I must not yet leave Vicarsfield: we lived, as I said, within a moving circle of enemies, who delighted to parade their formidable force: and our only earthly means of defence lay in the public knowledge of our being wholly unarmed, and without valuables in the house. The latter indeed were rarely sought; for it was a part of the system to prove to us that our lives, not our possessions, were the things thirsted after. Of this I will presently give a striking instance, which occurred in the house of another clerical friend.

The family party consisted of Dr. Hamilton, whose health was greatly affected by what he nevertheless endured with most uncomplaining meekness; Mrs Hamilton, struggling against her own strong feelings, and devoted to her husband and his guests: the curate, a most estimable young man; an aged field-officer of cavalry, whose military fire seemed to rekindle under the influence of the passing scene; a young lady resident in the house; with my mother and myself. A large establishment of domestics, male and female, and the thirteen girls of the school, with a superannuated serving-man who had seen two generations pass away, and whose eccentricities chiefly hinged on the most ardent orangeism imaginable, completed the garrison. Only three of the men besides "old John," viz: the coachman, butler, and footman, were quartered within doors, during the night, as being perfectly trustworthy; and no weapons, so far as we knew, did our little fortress contain, while it echoed to the shots fired in all directions by the marauding Rockites, the loud tramp of whose horses was likewise frequently audible through the stillness of the night. One instance I will give of the alarms to which we were subject.

We were all seated in the spacious drawing-room, on the
splendid organ of which Mrs. Hamilton had been performing
some of the finest of Handel's sublime compositions, until
summoned to preside at the tea-table. It was the middle of
February, and what with the elevating music, the cheerful
blaze of a good fire, and the conversation that always enli-
vened that pleasant hour, we were losing all recollection of
our peculiar circumstances, when suddenly, the loud jingle of
an alarm-bell sent a thrill to each heart, not easily to be
conceived by such as never dwelt in the midst of sanguinary
foes. A momentary pause of dead silence marked the effect of
that terrific note; the silence was unbroken, but immediately
after, the old Colonel, starting up, seized a large cane, as
though it had been a sword, and with energetic determination
speaking in his countenance marched to the door. The curate
passed after him; and Dr. Hamilton, with one look of stifled
anguish cast on us, then upturned to heaven, immediately
followed. We sate like statues, awe-struck, and mute, nor do I
think we should have attempted to move under anything that
might have ensued; but to our infinite relief one of the
servants came up, to express his regret that in bearing down
the large tea-tray he had inadvertently jarred one of the bells
on the staircase window-shutter. The incident, however, taught
us what before we had only imagined of our feelings under an
actual attack, and drew us nearer to him who alone is a sure
refuge in the day of calamity. We descended to the hall for
family worship, where, at a central point, Dr. Hamilton was
seated, with a little table before him, the family being ranged
along one division of the intersecting passages, the rest of the
household in the other. He read, expounded, and prayed; and
very touching was the silent "good night" *looked* between the
two divisions of the establishment. The respectful obeisance of
the faithful domestics, the kind recognition of those to whom
a fellowship in peril and in patience endeared them, spoke
much to all our hearts. Slowly and silently the young girls filed
off, conscious that the cabins of their friends were even then
lying at the mercy of those who were sworn to show no

mercy; and the sight of that little flock, all devoted to destruction, moved my heart as it never was moved under any other circumstances. Gladly would I undergo a repetition, yea an aggravation of all that then oppressed us, to enjoy once more the hallowed feelings of that time; when, with no help but what was unseen, no hope but in the God of martyrs, we trod on the very verge of eternity, in the pathway trodden by them.

Martyrdom indeed it was likely to be; for at this time accounts reached us of several, in our part of Ireland, having escaped death by their expertness in blessing themselves as it is called. This consists in making the sign of the cross with such rapidity and precision, in the established method, as practice alone can enable a person to use. This test was sometimes applied to distinguish any Romanist who might be in danger of suffering among Protestants, and now they had accepted it from some of the latter as a token of recantation. At breakfast, the next morning after our alarm, one of the party suggested sending for the gardener's wife to teach us the exact form of blessing ourselves after the Popish fashion; but I protested against it, as preparing a temptation that might overcome our constancy if called on to suffer for the truth. At first I was quite unsupported in the view; the rest saw nothing of a recantation in making a sign, to save our lives, which none of us would scruple to make as a matter of indifference. I could not yield the point: and the discussion that followed was on a question of life and death, impending directly over us. Scripture was mutually appealed to: Dr. Hamilton referred me to 1 Cor. viii, and I told him I was ready to let my argument stand or fall by that very chapter, as it proved that the sin did not consist in the act itself, but in the effect produced on weak brethren or unbelievers; that my making this sign at the demand of ignorant men, who would regard it as a real surrender of my faith, was as virtual an apostacy as if I signed a deed of recantation in the presence of the conclave. He seemed much startled, said he would take the subject into his study with him; and at the end of two hours I received a little note, written in a trembling hand, telling me that since I had led him to an investigation which had terminated in a full persuasion of mine being the right view of Scripture on this point, he hoped I would pray to the Lord to strengthen him and all of us that we might be found faithful until death, resisting even the semblance of compromise. He added that he had studied the matter on his knees and was then writing on his knees too. I was deeply affected on reading this; it was an awful thought that I stood responsible, in a measure, for the life-blood of my brethren; but the more I reflected, the clearer was my view of the subject, and to this day it remains unchanged.

The next night, Mrs. Hamilton was awakened by a loud and startling noise in the stables, which adjoined the house. An alarm was given to the servants; and one gallant young fellow, a footman, the Christian son of a truly Christianized convert from Popery, throwing on his great coat, and taking a lantern, darted out of the house alone, closing the door after him, which he could not have re-entered if attacked. The probability was that the horses were being abstracted for the service of Captain Rock, if nothing worse was going on: but it proved to be no more than the vicious gambols of a mule that had slipped the halter, and was invading the stalls of its quieter companions. You may suppose all this was trying enough, when accompanied by the echo of those shots that the midnight legislators systematically fired from all quarters to intimate their numbers and activity: yet if I were to declare at what period of my life I felt most calmly and happily resting on the arm of the Lord, I must say it was when laying my head on the nightly pillow which I knew might be steeped ere morning in my heart's blood. I could at any hour have returned to the comparative security of the populous town where I had a comfortable home; but the wish to avoid sharing the perils of those who had freely shared with me the sweets of their more prosperous hours, did not arise in my mind. One thing perplexed me greatly: in proportion as the native Irish became more terrible, as sanguinary bigots thirsting for our lives, so did my love for them increase. My Irish predilections had hitherto been merely confined to the higher classes; now they embraced every grade in society, and above all the miserable victims of Popish delusions excited my tenderest concern.

This was partly owing, no doubt, to a deeper insight into the infernal net that enclosed their souls. The more I learned of popery, the greater was my abhorrence of that gigantic Lie, and the yearnings of compassion over its unhappy slaves. Another cause may be found in my nearer acquaintance with the character of the people over whom I grieved. I lodged in the house of a rigid Romanist, who, with her family, partook in all the superstitions and prejudices of that system; yet sure I am that my own nearest connexions and oldest friends did not love me better, nor would have gone further to prove it, than that humble family. I very well knew that they must do the bidding of their spiritual despots, be it what it might, so far as God permitted; but their warmth of affection, their solicitude for our comfort, and feeling participation of all that touched us, whether of joy or sorrow, won my heart; and what they were I plainly saw to be the general character of their country-people.

Thus viewing the Irish as they really are, the most loving and loveable race under the sun, the most strongly inclined to devotedness, sincerity and zeal in whatever they believe to be truth, and shining most brightly as lights of the world, where what they have embraced is indeed the truth; how could my spirit fail to be stirred within me most earnestly on their behalf, when I saw from day to day, with my own eyes, the dreadful havoc of their bodies and souls made by the Antichristian enemy who had ensnared them? Taught from the cradle to regard as the arbiters of their present and eternal destiny, the men who made merchandize of them—assured that the priest could forgive their sins, or bind them irrevocably on their souls; could crown their dwelling with a blessing, or blast both it and them with a withering curse; could open to them the gates of heaven, or plunge them into the gates of hell; could transform, by means of a little unintelligible muttering, a cake perhaps of their own making, into the God who made them; or turn them, if he chose, into jackasses or goats, or wooden stools; could send them clean and holy out of the world by daubing them with a spoonful of oil, or by withholding it dismiss them to their account under a load of mortal sin; could release the soul of parent, wife, child, from a fiery purgatory by his masses, or keep them there as long as he listed (and who does not know that to the fond survivor of a beloved object *this* is the most adamantine chain of all?) and, finally, that to conceal from the aforesaid priest any thought of the heart, to resist his will in any particular, or to deny him the full measure of obedience due from man to God, is mortal sin:—taught to believe all this, from the earliest dawn of reason, the unhappy victim cannot deliver himself, nor say "Is there not a lie in my right hand?" Then, on the part of this omnipotent priesthood, what have we? not men zealous for the spread of the gospel, and the good of their poor flocks, but an associated band sworn to promote one object to the exclusion of all others; and that one the aggrandisement of their order, the supremacy of the Church, the extermination of true Christians, and universal extension of the temporal no less than the ecclesiastical empire of Rome over the whole earth. To the attainment of this end every means must be used: the mind of the disciple being wholly fettered, his hand must be directed to the deeds of blood against others, or his heart be pierced to pour forth his own, just as the interests of the great Satanic synagogue may at that moment require. This reads harshly; but it is a poor, weak, imperfect outline of what I have seen and grieved over from day to day, from year to year. I have conversed with these people while they were living in the most abject prostration of body, mind, and spirit before the merciless idol of their mistaken homage: I have seen the deluded soul passing into an unchangeable state of existence, under that awful malediction, "Cursed be he that trusteth in man; that maketh flesh his arm, and departeth from the living God." I have communed with those who by divine grace were delivered from the snare, and received their united testimony alike as to its power and its iniquity; and I have watched *their* dying beds, and almost always found them spending their last breath in thanksgivings for that mighty deliverance out of the chains of double darkness. I have traced the progress and effect of true religion in the minds of those emancipated children of God, and have marked how mighty for good is the natural, national character, which under this dreadful perversion has become so mighty for evil; and to crown all, I have been forced to recognize the sin of most cruel neglect and wrong on the part of my own country, in thus giving over the Irish race to the domination of present and eternal ruin. Principle and feeling alike plead the cause of poor Ireland: the plea reached my heart at the very time when, as I was told, I was specially noted for destruction among the anticipated victims of 1825, as being more than nominally a Protestant; and the atrocities that have marked the rapid development of plans first brought into operation at the time I have been speaking of, only add strength to my convictions; heightening my estimate of those who serve with such steadiness of purpose, the work which they, like Saul of Tarsus, ignorantly and in unbelief, consider most acceptable to God: and who, if brought into the way of righteousness, would be found, like Paul, labouring more abundantly in it than any of their brethren.

I cannot describe to you how this growing love for Ireland and the Irish ministered to my happiness. It became one of its chief elements; and the literary labour that I pursued for my own sustenance was perfect luxury, so long as my humble productions were made available for the spiritual good of the people so dear to me. My little books and tracts became popular; because, after some struggle against a plan so humbling to literary pride, I was able to adopt the suggestion of a wise Christian brother, and form a style of such homely simplicity, that if, on reading a manuscript to a child of five years old, I found there was a single sentence or word above his comprehension, it was instantly corrected to suit that lowly standard. This is an attainment much to be coveted by those who write, preach, or expound for general edification; no rational objection can be urged against it: vanity alone can enter a protest. Though our lettered readers or hearers may not find matter to gratify their taste, or pamper the pride of intellect, still they cannot fail to understand what is suited to the capacities of their children and servants; whereas he who makes himself perhaps both intelligible and agreeable to the former, is to the latter a barbarian, speaking in an unknown tongue; and what account will be given unto his Master of the souls that through his self-conceit, or neglectfulness of their peculiar deficiencies, remains unfed! How often has my heart been pained under the eloquent teaching of most gifted ministers, because I knew that many around me were wholly unable to attach a definite meaning to what he said, through the intervention of (to them) hard words and obscure phraseology. Thanks be to God, the translators of our blessed Bible were not of this school.

I had left Vicarsfield with feelings of increased affection for its inmates, and anxious solicitude as to their continued safety. In times of extreme peril, how much easier it appears to trust God with ourselves than with those whom we love? Personally, I was more than resigned: like a soldier entering the field of battle, I seemed nerved for the combat with a strength of purpose peculiar to the occasion; but looking on those who marched beside me, and scanning *their* dangers, fancying *their* sufferings, my courage would falter. This is Paul's meaning, when in reference to a "juncture" of peculiar trials just at hand, he seems to discourage the formation of ties which God has, under ordinary circumstances, ordained and blessed. It is not every woman who, like the wives of some of our blessed martyrs, can sit down to make for the beloved partner of her heart and life the garment in which he is to endure a terrible martyrdom; and then, with a train of helpless little ones at her heels, meekly present it at the gate of his prison. There must indeed be a full measure of grace conferred on both parties to enable each, in the calmness of resigned faith, to look in the sufferings of the other. Such grace may the Lord abundantly dispense to His people, now that a season of terrible trial is surely at hand!

Before closing this letter, I will relate an incident already
alluded to in proof of the assertion, that except on one single
point, there was little to dread from the agents of that wily
system which aimed at higher objects than mere plunder, or
isolated acts of violence. It occurred in the house of a most
intimate friend of ours, and I had it from the lady herself who
was exposed to that short but terrible alarm. Mr.——had
taken his whole family and household to the church of which
he was Rector, on the Sunday morning, with the sole exception of his wife's sister and his youngest babe, which she
remained at home to take care of. Miss——was sitting in the
parlour beside the cradle, reading her Bible, when a stir at the
door induced her to look round, and to her dismay six or
seven men appeared, the foremost of whom had opened the
door, and was in the act of entering. He seemed to belong to
the class of humble farmers; homely, but respectable, and his
manner bespoke great determination, softened with something of the courtesy which an Irishman finds it difficult to lay
aside in the presence of those who have not offended him. He
advanced to the trembling lady, and asked if there were any
fire-arms in the house? She replied, No! that her brother being
a clergyman, did not keep such weapons in his possession. To
this the visitor again answered that he must take the liberty of
searching for them, and would trouble her to conduct him
over the different parts of the house. Terrified, yet upheld by
a firm faith, the lady rose, took the unconscious babe from its
pillow, and wrapping her shawl round it, silently led the way
through adjoining apartments, the Rockites eagerly ransacking
every corner for arms, but without success. "Now, Ma'am, be
pleased to take us up-stairs," said the leader; and up stairs she
went, all following. On entering one of the rooms, she was
requested to unlock a chest of drawers; and the chief seeing
that she trembled greatly, said in a very decided tone, "I will
not have the lady frightened; back, all of ye, except you,"
addressing two near him, "and, Ma'am, don't be alarmed—
nobody wishes to hurt or distress you." The other men
retreated, and Miss——opened every drawer in that and the

other rooms, all of which, with the closets, were minutely inspected by the three searchers; who turned over articles of plate, money, and other valuables, without manifesting the slightest desire to appropriate one of them. The search was rewarded, I think, with no more than an old, useless blunderbuss, and rusty sword, with which they descended; and when again in the parlour the leader took off his hat, told Miss——— he was sorry to have alarmed her; he hoped he had made good his words that no harm was intended to her, and wishing her good morning, with a very polite bow, he retreated. She told me that after the first panic she scarcely felt discomposed, so much confidence did this man's manner inspire her with. Assuredly the Lord himself kept that house, while his dear servant was faithfully ministering to a little attached congregation on the mountain's side, and "stayed the rough wind in the day of his east wind" to the kind nurse and her helpless charge; but there is also something very striking in this conquest of poor and lawless men, alike over the cravings of avarice and those of vindictive hatred, with which they are sedulously taught to regard every professor of true Protestantism. They greatly err who attribute to personal hostility the outrages committed in Ireland: they are the deliberate execution of sentences formally passed by a secret Directory, on individuals far removed from the possibility of having excited such animosity in the bosoms of their unknown assassins, who are usually selected from districts the most remote; in order to avoid recognition, and to invest the work of murder with the air of a legal punishment in the eyes of those who commit it.

One more incident occurring within my immediate neighbourhood, I will relate. The victim was himself not only a Romanist, but brother to the person who assumed the title of Romish Bishop in that diocese. This Mr. Marum was a large farmer, possessing considerable property in land, near Kilkenny; and feeling more regard for his worldly possessions than interest in the cause of his religion, he discouraged the Rockite proceedings. Some great outrages having occurred, he represented to government the disturbed state of the

Barony, and induced them to send down a body of "Peelers," as the police were termed. This he knew to be an unpardonable offence, and therefore never went abroad unarmed; taking care to have it known that he did not.

One day he was riding with his son-in-law, at noon, and seeing some persons on the road before them, he turned round, saying, "I have forgotten my pistols; let us go back for them." The young man replied that it was not worth while; the distance was so short, and nobody near but a few women. This, with the appearance of the parties, attired in blue cloaks, and caps over which the hood was carelessly thrown, satisfied Marum; they proceeded at an easy pace, and had nearly passed the stragglers by the road-side, when a sudden rush was made upon them by the men, thus disguised for the purpose, and in a minute or two poor Marum lay on the ground, a murdered corpse. The son-in-law was knocked over senseless by a blow on the head from a stone, into a ditch, where he remained till succour came up. Of course, he was not sentenced, or they never would have left the work unfinished. A very great sensation was excited by this: his family connexion rendered Marum's murder a startling event to all parties; nor did it end here: he had another brother, a parish priest, who was believed to have aided him in preserving the public peace, and who strove anxiously to discover the murderers. After the inquest, a grand wake was held, at which this priest attended; and during his absence some unknown persons got into his small house, demolished all the furniture they could, turned every sod of grass in his field upside down, and carried off his cow. Here was sacrilege with a vengeance! and some simple people argued from it that religion had nothing to do with the political movement. True, in one sense, for Popery is not a religion—it is only a crafty piece of masked atheism, pursuing secular objects with a sanctified face; but Popery no more hesitates in cutting off a priest or making away with a pope who may fail in working out its arbitrary principles, than it shrinks from dethroning a king, or burning a Christian.

LETTER IX.

THE DUMB BOY.

The year 1824 was hailed throughout Ireland as one of confident hope, and active preparation for the great event that was to distinguish 1825—Protestant extermination. Black Lent was ordered to be kept, and extra masses celebrated, and special prayers for the destruction of heresy to be daily offered. These last were remarkably answered, for Popery never received such a blow in Ireland as followed the appeal. Encouraged by the implicit faith placed by the poor ignorant people in their blood-thirsty prognostics, the priesthood waxed bold, and resolved on making head against the encroachments of Christianity. Hitherto, a strict injunction had been laid on their flocks to abstain from entering any place of public meeting, held by the agents of the Bible and other religious societies: but now that the victim seemed within their grasp, they resolved to make sport with their captive Samson, and came forward themselves at Carlow and elsewhere, to oppose the Protestant clergymen; stationing a vast crowd of their followers in the rooms, well provided with the national weapon—the stem of a stout young oak or ash-tree, into the end of which, where the roots had been rounded off, a quantity of molten lead was poured, making the shillelagh more formidable in such hands than a sword would have been—much harder to parry, and impossible to break. In other places, the priests kept aloof, but sent their flocks to try the effect of these weighty arguments upon the heads of their Protestant neighbours. I will repeat the account given me, long afterwards, by a young man who attributed in great measure his subsequent conversion to one of these crusades.

"On the Sunday before, Father—— spoke to us all from the altar, and said, 'Boys, them Bible-men will hold a meeting here on Wednesday. You won't be going there to make a disturbance? you'll stay at home like peaceable people, and let them have things all their own way. I've heard it reported that some of you intend to go and have a scrimmage, but in course you have no such thing in your heads.' He spoke in such a sly way, that we all understood it, and laughed: however, if any spies were there, or if any mischief came of it, the entire of us could testify that Father—— had publicly warned his flock against taking part in it. Afterwards he spoke privately to about a dozen resolute boys, I being one, and told us to take our sticks and be there in good time. 'Break their heads if you can,' says he 'but any way drive them out of the town.'"

"Sure enough, we went: and I had as good a slip of blackthorn under my coat as you'd desire to see. The gentlemen mustered strong; Lord——, in the chair, looked as if he didn't feel quite at home; for, though he had often seen our faces before, it was not at Bible meetings. The Reverend Mr. Daly came forward; we had been recommended to look after him particularly, and so we would, but somehow he talked in such a way about Jesus Christ and the Bible, and God's love to sinners, that we disremembered every word of our instructions, and stood listening as if we had come there on purpose. By-and-by a bit of a spree *was* got up, but the boys had little heart to it, and it was easily put down. One thing I know for myself; and that is, that if we had come to blows, not a hair of *their* heads should have been hurt, and I standing by."

"And what did you do afterwards?"

"I went home and read the Bible."

Such were the effects of Pastorini's prophecy. It inspired one party with a false confidence that brought them to face the other, to whom God gave a mouth and wisdom such as their adversaries could neither gainsay nor resist. It issued in many conversions, and it gave the people a taste for controversial discussions, than which nothing can be better suited to their keen intellects, ready wit, and pugnacious propensities. At this gap, so inconsiderately made in the curtain, a flood of light streamed in; and the attempt to close it again was abortive. Never does God's providential sovereignty appear so glorious as when he thus makes the wrath of man to praise Him, and the devices of Satan to accomplish His own immutable designs.

In like manner, though on a smaller scale, the attack on my personal Protestantism was overruled to the gathering in of one precious soul to the true fold of Christ, and through him, I trust, very many more have been led to seek the same inestimable blessing. I turned my attention to the deaf and dumb children, whose situation was deplorable indeed; I took four out of the street to instruct them, of whom one proved irreclaimably wild and vicious; two were removed by a priest's order, lest I should infect them with heresy; the fourth was to me a crown of rejoicing, and will be so yet more at "that day."

I confess myself very little under the influence of human teachers: my being thrown exclusively on the Bible for a scheme of doctrine not only furnished me with a satisfactory one, but showed me so much of the inexhaustible treasures of wisdom and knowledge hid in Christ, and of the Holy Spirit's all-sufficiency to take of those things and shew them unto the humble, diligent, prayerful enquirer, that in most cases of difficulty, instead of asking, "What say the commentators?" or "what says Mr. so and so?" I put the question, "What says the LORD?" For an answer, I search his written word; and for a commentary upon it, I study his visible works. Now, the doctrine of personal election I know to be in the Bible, and I did not need man's confirmation to assure me that I had found it there; but it was delightful to witness such an illustration of that sublime truth as the case of the dumb boy in question afforded. He was the least promising of my little school, apparently the dullest, and certainly not the one on whom I bestowed the most pains; and who, after holding out strong encouragement, by his extraordinary quickness, brilliant talents, and devoted fondness to his instructor, merely served to introduce to me the poor little fellow whom he scarcely regarded as a companion; then forsook his post, cast off all rule, and, I fear, went on frowardly in the way of his own heart. It was not of him that willeth, nor of him that ran, but of God who showed mercy.

John, or Jack as we always called him, was a puny little fellow, of heavy aspect, and wholly destitute of the life and animation that generally characterize that class, who are obliged to use looks and gestures as a substitute for words. He seemed for a long while unable to comprehend my object in placing before him a dissected alphabet, and forming the letters into words, significant of dog, man, hat, and other short monosyllables; and when I guided his little hard hand to trace corresponding characters on the slate, it was indeed a work of time and patience to make him draw a single stroke correctly. His unmeaning grin of good-natured acquiescence in whatever I bade him do was more provoking than downright rebellion could have been; and I secretly agreed with my friends that the attempt would prove a complete failure, while impelled, I hardly could tell how, to persevere with redoubled efforts. Jack's uncouth, bristly hair, fell in a strait mass over one of the finest foreheads ever seen, and concealed it. I happened one day to put aside this mass, for the benefit of his sight, and was so struck with the nobly expansive brow, that I exclaimed to a friend then in the act of dissuading me from his work, "No! with such a forehead as this, I can never despair of success;" I was then anything but a phrenologist, for I erroneously looked upon it as leading to materialism; but experience had long taught me to regard that lofty feature of man's countenance as the just index of his intellectual capabilities.

It was by a sudden burst that the boy's mind broke its prison, and looked around on every object as though never before beheld, all seemed to appear in so new a light to him. Curiosity, in which he had been strangely deficient, became an eagerly active principle, and nothing that was portable did he fail to bring to me, with an enquiring shake of the head, and the word "What?" spelled by the fingers. It was no easy matter, when we had barely mastered a dozen common substantives, and no other parts of speech, to satisfy his inquisitiveness; which I always endeavoured to do, because it is wrong to repress that indication of dawning reason in a child, and Jack at eleven years old was in the predicament of a mere infant. More especially was I puzzled when his "what?" was accompanied by a motion pointing first at the dog, then to himself, to learn wherein consisted the difference between two creatures; both of whom, as he intimated, could eat, drink, sleep, and walk about, could be merry or angry, sick or well; neither of whom could talk; and yet that there was a very great difference, he felt. The noble nature of man was struggling to assert its pre-eminence over the irrational brute, which he nevertheless, loved and feared too; for Barrow was a splendid dog, and used to assist me very cleverly in keeping my little wild Irish crew in order. Oh what a magnificent wreck is man! I do love to watch the rapid approach of that glorious time when, the six thousand years of his degradation beneath the reign of Satan being fulfilled, he shall rise again in renovated majesty above the usurper's power, and resume his high station among the brightest works of God.

I do not remember exactly how long after his first coming to see me it was, that Jack began to inquire so diligently about God. He seemed full of grave, but restless thought, and then approaching me, pointed towards the sun, and by a movement of his hands, as if kneading something, asked me whether I made it. I shook my head. Did my mother?—No. Did Mr. Roe, or Mr. Shaw (the two Protestant clergymen) or the priest? He had a sign to express each of these.—No. Then, "What?—what?" with a frown and a stamp of fretful impatience. I pointed upwards, with a look of reverential solemnity, and spelled the word "God." He seemed struck, and asked no more at that time; but next day he overwhelmed me with whats, and seemed determined to know more about it. I told him as well as I could, that He of whom I spoke was great, powerful and kind; and that he was always looking at us. He smiled, and informed me that he did not know how the sun was made, for he could not keep his eyes on it; but the moon he thought was made like a dumpling, and sent rolling over the tops of the trees, as he sent a marble across the floor. As for the stars, they were cut out with a large pair of scissors, and stuck into the sky with the end of the thumb. Having thus settled his system of astronomy, he looked very happy, and patted his chest with evident self-applause.

I was amused, but of course not satisfied: my charge was necessarily an Atheist, and what I had told him was a very bare sort of Deism indeed. To communicate more, however seemed utterly impossible, until we should have accomplished considerable things in the way of education. We had not above a dozen of the commonest words—all names of things—to which he could attach a meaning; and our signs were all of his own contriving, which I had to catch, and follow as I might. So said Reason, but Reason is a fool. "Man shall not live by bread alone, but by every word that proceedeth out of the mouth of God doth man live." "For my ways are not your ways, neither are your thoughts my thoughts, saith the Lord." It pleased Him to enlighten the mind of the boy; and instead of that work being dependent on human wisdom, all that human wisdom could do was to creep after it, at a modest distance.

Next day, Jack came to me in great wrath, intimating that my tongue ought to be pulled out. This was his usual mode of accusation where a lie had been told. So I looked innocent and said, "What?" He reminded me of yesterday's conversation, telling me he had looked every where for God; he had been down the street, over the bridge, into the churchyard, through the fields, had peeped into the grounds of the castle, walked past the barrack-yard; and got up in the night to look out at the window. All in vain: he could not find God. *He saw nobody big enough to put up his hand and stick the stars into the sky.* I was "bad," my tongue must be pulled out; for there was "God No." And he repeated, "God—no!" so often that it went to my heart.

I considered, prayerfully. My view of the scriptures told me that without divine help none could really seek after God; and also that when he vouchsafed to give the desire, he would surely increase knowledge. Here was a poor afflicted boy, getting out of his bed to look by night for One whom he had vainly sought all the day; here was Satan at work to strengthen unbelief; I was commanded to resist the devil, and surely there must be some way of resisting him. I sat silent on the opposite side of the fire, and a plan having struck me, I looked at Jack, shrugged my shoulders, and seemed convicted of deception. He shook his head at me, frowned and appeared very much offended at my delinquency. Presently I seized a small pair of bellows, and after puffing at the fire for a while, suddenly directed a rough blast at his little red hand, which hung very near it. He snatched it back, scowled at me, and when again I repeated the operation expressed great displeasure, shivering, and letting me know that he did not like it.

I renewed the puff, saying, "What?" and looking most unconscious of having done anything; he blew hard, and repeated that it made his hands cold: that I was bad, and he was very angry. I puffed in all directions, looking very eagerly at the pipe of the bellows, peering on every side, and then, explaining that I could see nothing, imitated his manner, saying, "Wind—no!" shaking my head at him, and telling him his tongue must come out, mimicking his looks of rebuke and offended virtue. He opened his eyes very wide, stared at me, and panted; a deep crimson suffused his whole face, and a soul, a real soul shone in his strangely altered countenance, while he triumphantly repeated, "God like wind! God like wind!" He had no word for "like;" it was signified by holding the two forefingers out, side by side, as a symbol of perfect resemblance.

Here was a step, a glorious step, out of absolute atheism, into a perfect recognition of the invisible God. An idea, to call it nothing more, new, grand, and absorbing took possession of his mind. I numbered seven years of incessant care over him from that day; and I will fearlessly assert, that in his head and in his heart God reigned unrivalled. Even before he knew Him as God in Christ, the Creator and Preserver was enthroned in his bosom; and every event of the day, every object that met his view gave rise to some touchingly simple question or remark concerning God. He made me observe that when trying to look at the sun he was forced to shut his eyes, adding, "God like sun." An analogy not very traceable, though strictly just; for the glory that dazzled his mind was not visible. He was perpetually engaged in some process of abstract reasoning on every subject, and amazed me by explaining its results: but how he carried it on without the intervention of words, was and is a puzzle to me.

Previously he had been rather teasing to the dog, and other inferior creatures, and had a great desire to fish; but now he became most exquisitely tender towards every thing living; moving his hand over them, in a caressing way, and saying, "God made." At first he excepted the worms from this privilege remarking that they came up through holes from beneath the earth, while God was above over the sky; therefore they were not made by him; but I set him right, and he agreed that they might be rolled up in the world, like meat in a pudding, and bite their way out. Thenceforth woe to the angler whom Jack detected looking for live bait!

When my first pupil, from being irregular in his attendance, fell off more and more, until he wholly discontinued coming, and the others were withdrawn for fear of heretical infection, I became more anxious lest this dear boy might also leave me before he had received knowledge of Jesus Christ. I had at his earnest entreaty, taken him into the house altogether, his home being at some distance; but I knew not how long he might be permitted to stay. The ravages of a dreadful fever among the poor increased my solitude to see my devout little Deist a Christian. I have, in a small memoir of this "Happy Mute," related the manner of his receiving the Gospel, but I must not pass it over here. To the glory of God's rich grace it shall be recorded, as one of the most signal mercies ever vouchsafed to me. As before, the boy was led to open the way, and in the faith of the Lord's willingness to reveal himself to an enquiring soul, I followed it up.

Jack had noticed the number of funerals passing; he had occasionally seen dead bodies placed in their coffins; and one evening, he alluded to it, asking me by significant gestures if they would ever open their eyes again. Considering that he had often been present at the interment of the dead, and had also witnessed the decay of animals cast out to perish, it struck me as a singular question, plainly indicating that the consciousness of immortality is natural to man, and unbelief in a future state foreign to his untaught feelings. On the present occasion, my heart being even then lifted up in prayer for divine assistance on this very point, I caught at the encouragement, and instantly proceeded to improve the opportunity. I sketched on paper a crowd of persons, old and young: near them a pit with names issuing from it, and told him all those people among whom were we, had been "bad" and God would throw us into the fire. When his alarm was greatly excited, I introduced into the picture another individual, who I told him was God's Son; that he came out of heaven, he had not been bad, and was not to go into the pit; but that he allowed himself to be killed; and when he died, God shut up the pit; so the people were spared. This seemed to myself too strange, vague, meagre, to convey any definite idea to the boy's mind; but how effectual does the Lord make our poorest efforts when HE wills to work! After a few moments deep thought, Jack astonished me by an objection that proved he saw the grand doctrine of a substitute for sinners, which I was so hopeless of bringing before him. He told me the rescued people were many; he who died was one, and his earnest "What?" with the eloquent look that now peculiarly belonged to his once stupid countenance, showed his anxiety for a solution of this difficulty.

With unutterable joy in my heart, but great composure of manner, I rose, and taking from a vase a bunch of dead flowers, inadvertently left there, I cut them into small bits, laid them in a heap on the table, and beside them my gold ring:

then pointing to each, with the words "many—one," I asked which he would rather have? He struck his hand suddenly to his forehead, then clapped both hands, gave a jump as he sat, with the most rapturous expression of countenance, intimated that the one piece of gold was better than the room full of dead flowers. With great rapidity he applied the symbol, pointing to the picture, to the ring, to himself, to me, and finally to heaven. In the last position he stood up, and paused for some time, and what a picture he would have made! A smile perfectly angelic beaming on his face, his eyes sparkling and dancing with delight, until, with a rush of tears, that quite suffused them, he gazed at me, then again raised them to the ceiling, his look softened into an expression of deep awe, and unbounded love, while he gently spelled on his fingers, "good ONE—good ONE!" and ended by asking me his name.

> "How sweet the name of JESUS sounds
> To a believer's ear!"

Jack was not to hear that name with his bodily ears until the voice of the archangel and the trump of God should call his dust from sleeping in the earth; but he received it into his mind, and the Gospel, the glorious everlasting Gospel, into his soul, and the Holy Spirit into his heart, without the intervention of that sense. In the same hour it was given unto him to believe, and from that hour all things were his— the world, life, death, and a bright immortality. Never but once before had I laid my head on the pillow with such an overwhelming sense of perfect happiness. The Lord had indeed shown me His glory, by causing His goodness to pass before me.

Henceforth, I had a Christian brother in my little dumb charge; his love to Jesus Christ was fervent and full; his thoughts about him most beautiful. By degrees, I gave him some knowledge of our Lord's mortal birth, his infancy, work, death, resurrection and ascension; together with the future advent; which I then believed to be a coming to final judgment at the end of the world; and often was I puzzled by discerning that Jack had an impression on his mind of a coming to make his people happy here. At a time when I had never even heard of a personal reign, and he, to my certain knowledge, had no human teaching whatever except from me, at that time I am positively sure his views were those which I now hold; and I cannot account for it without looking higher than man.

Very great indeed was Jack's emotion, when he discovered that the Saviour in whom he was rejoicing was the object represented by the image he had been taught to bow down before. He resented it deeply: I was quite alarmed at the sudden and violent turn his feelings took against Popery. Awake as I was to its abominations, I yet temporized sadly in this matter; I had not faith to trust the Lord with his own; and dreading lest any interference with the forms of their idolatrous worship should cause his friends to take him from me, as Pat must have known it immediately, I refrained from approaching the subject, and allowed the poor little fellow to bow down with the rest in a mass-house. If I ever was tempted to believe, which I never am, that God leaves any of his own children in the communion of Antichrist, Jack's case would effectively rebuke me: he spurned the whole system from him, in spite of me, as soon as the light of the gospel fell upon its deformities.

Returning from chapel, one day, soon after this, he came up to me, under great excitement: he took up a clothes-brush, set it on one end, and with ludicrous grimace bowed down before it, joining his hands in the attitude of prayer, and chattering after his fashion; he then asked the brush if it could hear him, waiting in an attitude of attention for its reply, and finally knocked it over, and kicked it round the room, saying "Bad god, bad god!" I guessed pretty well what it was all about; but as he concluded by snapping his fingers exultingly, and seating himself without further remark, I spoke on other subjects. My feelings were far from enviable.

Next morning, Jack was very animated, and came to me with an evident budget of new thoughts. He told me something very small came out of the ground, pointing in opposite directions; it grew; and then two more points appeared. I found he was describing the growth of a plant, and expecting some question, was all attention; but Jack was come to teach not to learn. He soon showed that his tree had reached a great height and size; then he made as if shouldering a hatchet, advanced to the tree, and cut it down. Next came a great deal of sawing, chopping, planning and shaping, until he made me understand he had cut out a crucifix, which he laid by, and proceeded to make a stool, a box, and other small articles; after which he gathered up the chips, flung them on the fire, and seemed to be cheering himself in the blaze. I actually trembled at the proceeding; for where had he, who could not form or understand half a sentence, where had *he* learned the Holy Spirit's testimony as recorded by Isaiah?

The sequel was what I anticipated: he feigned to set up the imaginary crucifix, and preparing to pray before it, checked himself, saying, "No:" then with animated seriousness reverted to the springing up of the little seedling, saying, "God made;" and as it grew, he described the fashioning of the trunk and branches, and leaves, most gracefully, still saying "God made:" he seemed to dip a pencil in colour, to paint the leaves, repeating "God made beautiful!" Then he signified that God made his hands too, and he came to the conclusion that the tree which God made, cut out by his hands which God made, could be not God who made them. Then he got very angry and not satisfied with an insubstantial object for his holy indignation to vent itself upon, he ran for the clothes-brush and gave it a worse cuffing and kicking than before; ending with a solemn enquiry, whether I worshipped crosses, &c., when I went to church?

How guilty I felt! and still I trembled to give the encouragement I longed to bestow. However, I distinctly intimated my detestation of idolatry, and confirmed his strong repudiation of it. He told me he would not go any more to chapel. But I told him, as well as I could, the almost certain consequences, and he then remembered that other boys had told him those who ate meat on Fridays would go to hell; and that the same people were to be killed; for this was in 1824, and Pastorini was universally quoted. He became greatly distressed as the next sabbath approached, but contrary to all my expectations returned from mass in excellent spirits. Pat told me, laughing, that Jack was become so musical he insisted on going to sit by the organ, that he might feel the vibration; and when alone with me, Jack joyfully told me that he had run up the stairs from the outer door to the organ-loft, and so escaped even the necessity of bowing down to the cross. This plan he persisted in from that day. Some years afterwards I asked his brother if he had any suspicion at the time of the boy's object in so doing: he answered, None at all; and that if he had he would have forced him into the body of the mass house and compelled him to prostrate himself.

May the Lord grant that what I have thus narrated may be made the means of conveying a lesson to every reader! It was one of the great commendations of the Church at Ephesus that they hated the deeds of the Nicolaitans, which Christ also hates; and let us daub over our indifference as we may with the false varnish of liberality, charity, and so forth, it will be an awful item against our souls if we do not hate, actively hate, the deeds of Antichristian Rome; and prove it by exposing the vile snare, that we may deliver those whom it holds captive. We have fritted away God's truth, and well night trampled out his line of demarcation, between a holy worship and the polluted sacrifice of an idol-temple, while speculating on the fair front of Jansenism as opposed to Jesuitism: we have turned from the fires of Smithfield to contemplate the well-told tales of Port-Royal, and thrust our Bradfords, our Latimers, yea and our Luthers from the shelf, to set up Fenelon and à Kempis. To their own master they stood or fell. Fenelon's appointed work was the conversion of Protestants to Popery; he used all the influence of his very superior mind and amiable character to draw the persecuted Huguenots into communion with Rome. It was his glory that he succeeded so far, and no doubt he did it conscientiously; but so long as I read in my Bible

that Satan transforms himself *into an angel of light* to seduce
Christ's servants from their allegiance to HIM, I will not
tamper with my faith by sitting down to ascertain how much
of Christianity I can discover in certain individuals who
actively promoted a system against which the God of heaven
had pronounced an irrevocable, a withering, and a final curse.

A dreadful instance occurring in our immediate neighbourhood about this period, manifested more alarmingly than
ever the perilous excitement of the poor people's minds, on
whom the wicked predictions already noticed had taken
effect. Not more than a quarter of a mile from the barracks
of Kilkenny lived a family of unoffending, respectable
Protestants, named Marr. One Sunday afternoon, long before
sunset, while they were sitting round the tea-table with unfas-
tened doors, a party of Rockites rushed into the house, loudly
demanding arms. The father and his eldest son ran up stairs,
probably intending to make some defence; but it was too late,
so they brought down what weapons they had, and delivered
them up. The intruders turned to go; but first opened the parlour door, where the rest of the family remained, panic-struck
and perfectly quiet; and one of them taking deliberate aim at
the second son, a peculiarly harmless character because he
was of weak intellect, with the manners of a little child, shot
him. The bullet entered just above his elbow; and as he fell, the
murderous aggressor made off, laughing, with his companions.

The young man was brought into Kilkenny, and most
assiduously attended by the medical gentlemen, while the
clergyman of our parish and his brethren in the ministry
were constantly engaged in prayer beside him, or in soothing
the anguish of his mother and sisters. The ball could not
be extracted, neither could the bleeding by any means be
staunched; but drop by drop, in lingering agony, the vital
current escaped from the youth's veins, and he was several
days dying. Outside the window of the house assembled a
number of women from the lowest class of the Romish population, and there they sate, responding with a yell of triumph
to every groan the poor sufferer uttered, praying that he

might have smart enough before he went; and shouting
"You'll be in hell presently, you Protestant locust, and then
you'll cry louder:" and with similar exclamations, and most
awful curses on the whole race. Why were they not removed?
you will ask, but who was to remove them? Were 24,000 people
to be roused into open violence, with a couple of Highland
companies in garrison, and a small force of Police, and 800
terrified Protestants, fully aware that at the first intimation of
an outburst fifty or a hundred thousand armed foes would
pour in from the surrounding country? No: the outcries of a
few wretched women were not to produce that effect, though
probably it was calculated upon; and the innocent victim died
amid their shouts. I remember one of the clergymen came to
me, requesting a glass of wine, and bursting into a passion of
tears as he recounted what he had heard, while praying in the
midst of that agonized family, as the spirit of the murdered
youth departed with a long deep groan that extorted a scream
of joy from the eager listeners without. I can fancy you here
pausing, to ask if I could love such a savage crew? Not those
individuals certainly, as then engaged; but I looked beyond
the hateful fruit to the execrable root that bore it, and felt
how terrible our own responsibility in that we had not laid the
axe to it while yet the opportunity was given, by preaching
Popery out of Ireland, by the same means that banished it from
England and Scotland. There was nothing in this demon-
stration inconsistent with the usual workings of that ferocious
persecutor all over the world. The records of Piedmont bear
a testimony to which all lands in all ages sent forth a corro-
borative voice, that where Popery has gained the ascendant
the demons of cruelty rage uncontrolled, so long as a whisper
or look dissentient from its dogmas may be detected: nay, we
well know that infancy, and as in the case just cited, imbecility
of mind, where neither assent nor dissent can be traced,
comes under the murderous ban. That human beings can
always be found to execute these frightful behests is a
lamentable, a humiliating fact; but when once given over to
a reprobate mind, of what is man not capable?

While these things were going on, many of the principal sufferers from them, consoled themselves under the persuasion that what they were enduring would turn to the good of the Protestant cause, by convincing the government how utterly vain was any hope of transforming Popery into a peaceable neighbour by any further concessions. Every one knew that the "emancipation" so loudly called for, could work no other change in the hostile party than as it must afford them an important step in advance to final ascendancy. What could such concessions do in neutralizing the effect of Pastorini's prophecies?

Would the "locusts" cease to be so by bestowing a tardy boom on the Romanists, wrung from them at the pike's point? It seemed impossible that any statesman should fall under such infatuation; and we were glad to see the mask so entirely thrown off, though our own proximity to the unveiled abomination rendered it trying to us. Most assuredly the Protestants of Ireland were not consenting to that deed: some, dwelling in secure cities, and wholly careless whether truth or falsehood ruled the realm, joined the cry of liberalism; and others in exposed situations forebore to utter their sentiments at all, well-knowing that every word spoken in the hearing of their Romish domestics would speedily find its way to the confessional; but in general there was a firm, undisguised opposition to the surrender of the national faith; and sure I am that the Protestants of Ireland never acquiesced in having *their* dangers made the plea for throwing down the bulwarks of the constitution.

Early in the summer of 1824, I received a summons to return to England. It was most unwelcome, for my heart was knit to Ireland, and to share the lot of her devoted people was its earnest desire. At home I had many old friends; but what were they to the beloved brethren and sisters in Christ who had been my fellow-helpers in the work of the Lord for the last four years? All ties were weak to that, save one—the tie that bound me to my beloved brother. Him I had not seen for nine years: he had continued on the staff of the Portuguese army until the establishment of the Cortes, who dismissed all

British officers; and then he settled in the interior of the country, cultivating some of the land which he had gallantly fought to rescue. It was a subject of continual sorrow to me that he was residing in the heart of an exclusively Popish country, far from every means of grace; not even a place of worship within many leagues, and wholly shut out from Christian intercourse. I knew that he had been equally dark with myself on the subject of religion, and truly can I say that from the very hour of my being enabled to see the truth as it is in Jesus, my life had been a constant prayer for him, that God would make him a partaker in the like precious faith. There was now a prospect of his returning, and this, added to the summons I have mentioned, made my way plain. The state of Jack's feelings too, on the subject of Popery, helped to reconcile me, since I had made up my mind to take him with me if his parents would agree to it. There was no difficulty in bringing them to do so; they gave a willing, a grateful consent. His mother's words, while tears rolled down her cheeks, were, "Take him; he is more your child than our's." His father remarked, "Why shouldn't we let him go with you, seeing he would grieve to death if you left him behind?" When I began to state that I could not promise he would not openly embrace my religion, they interrupted me, repeating that he was my child more than their's, and could never come to any harm under my care. Coward as I was, I did not use the opportunity then given to set before them their own danger, and commend the pure faith that I knew their child held. I had occasionally talked in a general way, and once very strongly when the mother told me of the dreadful penances she had done, walking on her bare knees over a road strewed with pebbles, glass, and quick-lime, to make her sufferings greater, in order to obtain from God and the saints the restoration of the boy's hearing and speech. She was then pleading the power and holiness of her clergy, and their superiority to all the rest of the world. I looked from the window, and said, "See, there goes your bishop; now do you think this bright sun warms him more than it does any Protestant walking beside him?" "Troth, and I am sure it does!" answered she. "What, do you think he has any particular advantage over other men in things that are common to all?" "That he has, being a holy bishop." "Well, now, if I call him up, and we put all our fingers together between these bars, do you think the fire would burn him less than us?" She hesitated; her husband burst into a laugh; and archly said, "I'll engage his reverence wouldn't try that same."

I was now to bid adieu to my pleasant haunts; chief among which was the lordly castle of Kilkenny, where I had passed so very many delightful hours. Its noble owners were abroad, but by their favour I had a key to the private door beside the river, and full access to every part of the castle and its beautiful grounds. It was there I used to muse on days of Ireland's bygone greatness, though not then well-read in her peculiar history, and gradually I had become as Irish as any of her own children. How could it be otherwise? I was not naturally cold-hearted, though circumstances had indeed greatly frozen the current of my warm affections, and I had learned to look with comparative indifference on whatever crossed my changeful path; but no one with a latent spark of kindly feeling can long repress it among the Irish. There is an ardour of character, an earnestness in their good-will, a habit of assimilating themselves to the tastes and plans of those whom they desire to please—and that desire is very general—that wins, in the affections of those who possess any, a grateful regard, and leaves on the scenes that have witnessed such intercourse, a sunshine peculiar to themselves. Reserve of manner cannot long exist in Irish society: I have met with some among the people of the land, who were cold and forbidding, insensible and unkind, but these were exceptions, establishing the rule by the very disagreeable contrast in which they stood out from all around them: and I never found these persons in the humbler classes, where the unmixed Irish prevails. Hospitality is indeed the pole-star of Ireland; go where you will it is always visible: but it shines the brightest in the poor man's cabin, because the potato that he so frankly, so heartily, so

gracefully presses upon your acceptance, is selected from a
scanty heap, barely sufficient to allay the cravings of hunger
in himself and his half-clad little ones. In this as in all other
particulars a change for the worse has come over the people
of late; priestly authority has interposed to check the out-
goings of kindness, from a warm-hearted people to those who
are indeed their friends, and a painful, reluctant restraint is
made upon them; but the evil had not become evident at the
time of my sojourn there, and I can only speak of them as the
most respectful, most courteous and most hospitable peasantry
in the world. At the same time they were in many respects the
most degraded. Nothing could equal the depth of their abase-
ment before an insolent priesthood, except the unblushing
effrontery with which the latter lorded it over them. For any
infraction of their arbitrary rules, the most cruel and humiliating penances were imposed. I knew an instance of a young
woman, a Romanist, who engaged in the service of a Protestant
family, and went out with them to America. While there, she
was led to join in family worship, but without any intention
of forsaking her own creed; neither had they attempted to
draw her out of the net. On her return to Kilkenny she went
to confession, and among other things divulged the fact of
having heard the bible read, and having prayed in company
with heretics. This was an enormity too great for the priest to
deal with alone; so he ordered the girl off, fasting, to her
original confessor, who then officiated in a chapel seven good
Irish miles distant. On hearing the case, he ordered her to go
thrice round the chapel on her bare knees, and then to set off,
still fasting, and walk back to Kilkenny, there to undergo such
additional penance as his reverend brother should see good to
impose. The poor creature scarcely reached the town alive,
through fatigue, exhaustion, and terror; she was ill for some
time, and on her recovery was subjected to farther discipline.
These particulars I had from one of her own friends, and a
bigotted papist to boot, who told it in order to convince me
that the girl had committed a very great sin. I once asked a
young man how he got on at confession—whether he told all

his sins. He replied, "Sometimes I disremember a few; and if the priest suspects it, he pulls my hair and boxes my ears to help my memory." "And how do you feel when you have got absolution?" "I feel myself all right: and I go out and begin again." "And how do you know that God has really pardoned you?" "He doesn't pardon me directly: only the priest does. He (the priest) confesses my sins to the bishop, and the bishop confesses them to the pope, and the pope sees the Virgin Mary every Saturday night, and tells her to speak to God about it." "And you really believe this monstrous story?" "Why shouldn't I? But it is no affair of mine: for, once I have confessed, all my sins are laid on the priest, and he must do the best he can to get rid of them:—I am safe." Of such materials is the net composed that holds these people in bondage: and who can marvel that such prostration of mind before a fellow mortal should lead to an abject slavery of the whole man, body, conscience, and understanding? We see the effects and abhor them: but we do not go to the root of the matter. The priest himself is equally enslaved: his oath binds him to an implicit, blind reception of tenets which he is not permitted to investigate, and which make him the pliant tool of a higher department of this detestable machinery. He receives his cue from the bishops, and they are wholly governed by the Propaganda at Rome, where each of them is bound periodically to appear, for personal examination and fresh instructions. The Propaganda is, of course, the *primum mobile* of the system, set a-going by Satan himself. Hence the mischief that is perpetrated by the unhappy beings who form the operative section of this cunning concern: the handicraft men of blood. It is an awful spectacle, and one that we cannot long avert our eyes from contemplating with the deep interest that personal peril excites. All is preparing for a burst of persecution against the people of the Lord, and happy is he who shall be found armed and watching!

LETTER X.

ENGLAND.

We started for Dublin with sorrowing hearts, for it was likely to be a long if not a last farewell to friends who were endeared as well by a participation in danger as in feeling. Those who have daily been expecting to die together in a holy cause, cannot lightly part. One of the last things that I learned, before leaving the place, was communicated to me by an intimate friend and near neighbour, a very sweet Christian character. She had lived on terms of intimacy with a Romish family in the town, and a few days previous to my departure the mother of this family called on Miss——, with tears entreating her to embrace Popery; for that the next year would witness the utter extermination of Protestants, and it would be out of her power, or that of any other person, to save any life, however dear to them. She urged it with most affectionate importunity, and was evidently much distressed at her failure. Whether the better-informed class of the Romanists believed in Pastorini's prediction or not, they saw them universally received among the bulk of the people, and of course knew that they would take care to verify what they believed. It was by a wonderful interposition that the Protestants of Ireland were saved, though an unmarked one; for with a population of six to one, roused to the highest pitch of religious fanaticism, prepared by extra masses, fasts, and prayers, and confiding in the assurance of an infallible church that so it must be——where, too, they had every thing to gain and little or nothing to lose——it is marvellous that such a restraint was laid on their sanguinary purposes. The priestly fancy of entering into discussion with their opponents wrought powerfully against their own cause; and the notorious Doyle, who led the way in every species of agitation and mischief, and sanctioned the riotous meeting at Carlow, one of the ablest, wiliest and boldest of Romish bishops, whose writings were firebrands, and who in a public speech eulogized a farmer in his diocese for taking the Bible in the tongs and burying it in a hole in his garden—that Dr. Doyle afterwards died a Protestant; nor could all the devices of his brethren long conceal the fact.

Jack had never before been beyond the environs of his native town, and I expected to see him much astonished by the splendid buildings of Dublin. He regarded them, however, with indifference, because, as he said, they were not "God-mades," while the scenery through which he had travelled, particularly the noble oaks in Colonel Bruen's fine demesne, and the groups of deer reclining beneath their broad shadow, roused him to enthusiasm. It was wonderful to trace the exquisite perception of beauty as developed in that boy, who had never even been in a furnished room until he came to me. His taste was refined, and his mind delicate beyond belief: I never saw such sensitive modesty as he manifested to the last day of his life. Rudeness of any kind was hateful to him; he not only yielded respect to all, but required it towards himself, and really commanded it by his striking propriety of manner. He was, as a dear friend once remarked, a "God-made" gentleman, untainted with the slightest approach to anything like affectation or coxcombery: indeed he ridiculed the latter with much comic effect; and the word "Dandy Jack" would put him out of conceit with any article of apparel that drew forth the remark. He would answer the taunt with a face of grave rebuke, saying, "Bad Mam, bold Mam; Jack dandy, no: Jack, poor boy." He had not, indeed, arrived at so copious a vocabulary when he left his home; but he was rapidly acquiring new words.

It was beautiful to see him at prayer: he had never kneeled down with us in Kilkenny; for any Romanist who had detected him doing so must have informed, and the priest would have commanded his removal. In Dublin he volunteered to join us, and as he kneeled with clasped hands, looking up towards heaven, the expression of his countenance was most lovely. A smile of childlike confidence and reverential love played over his features, now becoming most eloquent; his bristly hair had begun to assume a silky appearance, and was combed aside from a magnificent brow, while a fine colour perpetually mantled his cheeks, and changed with every emotion; his dark hazle eyes, large, and very bright, always speaking some thought that occupied his mind. He was rather more than twelve years old. In profile he much resembled Kirke White when older; but the strongest likeness I ever saw of his is an original portrait of Edward VI., by Holbein, in my possession. It was taken after consumption had set its seal on the countenance of that blessed young king, as it did on that of my dear dumb boy.

One adventure he had in Dublin that afforded him much enjoyment. I went into an extensive toy-shop to make some purchases, and Jack, enchanted with the wonders around him, strolled to the further end, and into a little adjoining recess, well filled with toys. A great uproar in that direction made us all run to inquire the cause, and there was Jack, mounted on a first-rate rocking horse, tearing away full gallop, and absolutely roaring out in the maddest paroxysm of delight, his hat fallen off, his arm raised, his eyes and mouth wide open, and the surrounding valuables in imminent peril of a general crash. The mistress of the shop was so convulsed with laughter that she could render no assistance, and it was with some difficulty I checked his triumphant career, and dismounted him. He gave me afterwards a diverting account of his cautious approach to the "good horse," how he ascertained it was "bite, no; kick, no;" and gradually got resolution to mount it. He wanted to know how far he had rode, and also if it was a God-made? I told him it was wood, but I doubt whether he believed me. Thenceforth Dublin was associated in mind with nothing else: even at nineteen years of age, he would say, if he met with the name, "Good Dublin, good horse; small Jack love good Dublin horse." The shipping pleased him greatly, and many of his beautiful drawings were representations of sailing-vessels.

I had now been in Ireland five years and three months; and with what different feelings did I prepare to leave its green shores from those with which I first pressed them! Unbounded prejudice was succeeded by an attachment based on close acquaintance with those among whom I had dwelt; contempt by respect, and dislike buy the warmest, most grateful affection. I had scorned her poverty, and hated her turbulence. The first I now knew to be no poverty of soil, of natural resources, of mind, talent or energy; but the effect of a blight, permitted to rest alike on the land and people, through the selfishness of an unjust, crooked policy, that made their farewell of no account in its calculations, nor would stretch forth a hand to deliver them from the dark dominion of Popery. Their turbulence was the natural fruit of such poverty, and of their being left wholly under the influence of a party necessarily hostile to the interests of a Protestant state, and bent on subverting its ascendancy. What Ireland was, I too plainly saw; what she might be, I clearly understood: and the guilt of my country's responsibility lay heavy on my heart, as I watched the outline of her receding coast.

Bristol was our destination: and for the ensuing year, Clifton became our abode. The period of my life was one of severe trial, which it is not necessary to particularize. Incipient derangement, which afterwards became developed, in a quarter where, if I did not find comfort and protection, I might expect their opposites, occasioned me much alarm and distress, while my brother's protracted absence increased the trial. Much secluded, I pursued my literary avocations, and watched the progress of Jack's growth in knowledge and in grace.

Clifton is certainly one of the most beautiful spots in England: the river winding its graceful way beneath St. Vincent's picturesque rocks on the one side, and on the other the noble plantations of Leigh rising, as it were, out of the water, and overhanging it with grove and garden, is enchanting; while the constant succession of vessels of every variety of size and character, passing to and fro, fills the mind with a picture of commercial greatness, the more striking from its locality. The number of steamers was then small; the ungraceful chimney, with a long pennon of black smoke, had not superseded the tapering mast and swelling sails, nor given a hurrying rapidity to the slow, gliding movement so peculiar to a ship in smooth water. Every one of these sea-kettles ought to be inscribed with the motto, "Death to the picturesque." They now send their dark vapours curling up St. Vincent's cliffs, and by continually agitating the waters destroy the transparency of that elegant river. But believing, as I do, that these "swift messengers" have a special commission, in the divine purpose, to bring from all parts of the world that acceptable present unto the Lord of Hosts—his own peeled and scattered Israel—to the holy mountain of Jerusalem, I am reconciled to the temporary sacrifice of effect, as I should indeed be to the sacrifice of all earthly good, in the prospect of that blessed event. Every steamer launched, every rail laid down in the highways, is a step towards the accomplishment of those glorious things that are promised to crown the tribulation of these latter days; and while Satan will doubtless avail himself of them for cruelty, and devastation, they shall ultimately fulfil all the Lord's pleasure, when he says to Jerusalem, "Thou shalt be built," and to Zion, "Thy foundations shall be laid."

My sojourn at Clifton brought me into personal acquaintance with that venerable servant of God, Hannah More. We had for some time corresponded, and she had afforded me great encouragement in my humble labours, taking an especial interest in my attempts to instruct the deaf and dumb children. I had now the pleasure of showing her the progress made with Jack, who delighted her greatly, and who, to the last day of his mortal existence, most fondly cherished the memory of that sweet old lady. She was, indeed, one of the excellent of the earth, permitted long to beautify the church which she

had so mainly helped to strengthen and advance, and to be
an honour to the land where she had nobly stood forth to
repel the assaults of revolutionizing impiety. I often wonder
that so little stress is laid upon this branch of Mrs. More's
extensive labours. We hear much of her schools, her charities,
her letters, her devotional and educational publications, and
all of these deserve the full celebrity that they have attained.
But England should especially bear in mind her effective
championship of the good cause, by means most admirably
adapted to its furtherance among the most dangerous, and,
generally speaking, the most unapproachable class—a class
who congregated in ale-houses to hear the inflammatory
harangues of seditious traitors, while as yet Bibles were scarce,
religious tracts not in existence, and district-visiting unthought
of. In a lady of refined taste, and rare accomplishments in the
higher style of writing, to volunteer in a work so new, and to
furnish the press with a series of plain truths, dressed in most
homely phrase, rendered attractive by lively narrative and
even drollery, and the whole brought down to the level of
coarse, uninformed minds, while circulated in a form to come
within the narrow means of the lowest mechanics—this was
an enterprise worthy especial note, even had not God openly
blessed it to the turning of that formidable tide. When I gazed
upon the placid but animated countenance of the aged saint,
as she sat in her bow-window looking out upon the fair fields,
the still inviolate shores of her beloved country, I thought
more of her "Cheap Repository Tracts" than of all her other
works combined. There lay the Bristol Channel, that noble
inlet of our isle, by which the commerce of the world was
even then finding its peaceful way to the great mart of Bristol;
and there sat the aged lady, so long the presiding spirit of the
place, with one hand as it were gathering the lambs of the
flock into green pastures among the distant hills, that formed
a beautiful feature in the landscape; with the other vigorously
repulsing the wolf from the field. If I could have discovered,
which I could not, a single trait of consciousness that she was
a distinguished being, exalted into eminence by public acclaim,

I must have conceived her to be dwelling upon this branch of her many privileges, that she had been a Deborah when many a Barak shrunk from the post of honour, and skulked behind a woman. She took that lively interest in the public, secular affairs of her country that Jeremiah and Ezekiel did of old, and on the same plain ground: that where the state professes to be modelled, and the executive to act, on principles of God's instilling, with a view that peace and happiness, truth and justice, religion and piety, may be established among us, nothing done by the state can be indifferent to the church, or unworthy the anxious, watchful regard of Christians. To be called a carnal politician by those whose minds, at least on religious subjects, could contain but one idea, was certainly a light affliction to balance against the joyous consciousness of having materially aided in preserving those cavillers' homes from the hand of the spoiler, and their Bibles from that of the Atheist.

When I saw Hannah More she was really at ease in her possessions; and none who loved her less than the Lord himself did would have laid a sorrow upon her grey hairs. Man would have decreed, that such a full-ripe shock of corn should be brought into the garner without further ruffling or shaking. She had suffered exceedingly from rheumatism and other ailments, and yet more from the tongue of calumny, and the hand of ingratitude. She was an illustration of that striking couplet,

> "Envy will merit as its shade pursue,
> And, like the shadow, proves the substance true."

She had, however, triumphed over all, by meekly committing her cause to him who judgeth righteously; and now she seemed to be placed beyond the reach of further molestation; and about to end her useful life in peace. But she had another lesson to give to the people of God, another fire in which to glorify him; and not long after I saw her reclining in that lovely retreat which had grown up about her, a perfect bower from slips and seeds of her own planting, as she delighted to tell us, she was actually driven out of her little paradise, compelled to leave the shadow of her nursling trees, and to cast a tearful farewell look on the smiling flowers, and to turn away from the bright sea, and the waving line of her Cheddar hills, to find a lodging in the neighbouring town; and all through treachery, domestic treachery, against her whose whole life had been a course of unsparing beneficence towards others! Hannah More, perhaps, needed to be again reminded, that she must do all her works "as to the Lord," looking to him alone for acceptance of them; or if she needed it not, others did; and often since she entered into her Saviour's presence, "to go no more out," has the scene of the last trial to which her generous, confiding, affectionate spirit was subjected, been blessed to the consolation of others. God's children find that it is good for themselves that they should be afflicted; but they do not always remember how good it is for the church that they should be so. They look within and seeing so much there daily, "justly deserving God's wrath and condemnation," they lie still in his hand, willing and thankful to have the dross purged out, and all the tin taken away. Their fellows look on, and not seeing the desperate wickedness of their hearts, but fondly believing them to be as near perfection as human frailty will permit, they argue, "If such a saint as —— be thus chastened and corrected, what must a sinner like me expect!" So they learn watchfulness and fear in the day of prosperity; and when adversity comes, they are enabled more lovingly to kiss the rod. Oh, if we could see but a little of the Lord's dealings, in all their bearings, how should we praise him for his goodness, and the wonders that he doeth unto the children of men! What profit, what pleasure has He in afflicting us? Surely it is, so to speak, more trouble to correct than to leave us alone; and he would not twine the small cords into a scourge unless to cleanse and sanctify his temple.

I have said that my brother's return home was delayed. A hurt received in shooting, with its consequences, detained him in Lisbon nearly a year; but his family came over, and I had a new, delicious employment, a solace under many sorrows, an unfailing source of interest and delight, in teaching his eldest surviving boy the accomplishments of walking and talking. I almost expected Jack to be jealous of such a rival, but I wronged him: nothing could exceed his fondness for "Baby boy," or the zeal of his Irish devotion to the little gentleman. Knowing that in the event of my removal, Jack must earn his bread by some laborious or servile occupation, I had kept him humble. He ate in the same room with us, because I never suffered him to associate with servants; but at a side-table: and he was expected to do every little household work that befitted his age and strength. A kind shake of the hand, morning and evening, was his peculiar privilege; and the omission a punishment too severe to be inflicted, except on occasions of most flagrant delinquency, such as rebelling against orders, or expressing any angry emotions to which he was constitutionally liable, by yells and howls that almost frightened the Hot-wells from their propriety. He had, of course, no idea of the strength of his own lungs, nor of the effect produced by giving them full play in a fit of passion; but the commotion into which it threw the whole house seemed to flatter his vanity, and he became a vocalist on very trifling occasions. This neither agreed with our dear invalid landlady, nor was a fitting example for "Baby boy," who speedily tried his own little treble in admiring imitation of Jack's deafening bass; and recourse was at last had to the aid of a young friend, who bestowed a few gentle raps on his head with the bent end of a hooked cane, and then locked him up in a dark kitchen for half an hour, saying to me, rather regretfully, "I suppose my popularity is at an end now. Poor fellow! I shall be sorry to lose his affection." But this was so far from being the case, that to his closing scene Jack retained a grateful remembrance of the proceeding. He used to say, "Good Mr. W.; good little stick beat Jack's head; made bad Jack good. Jack love good Mr. W." At the very time, as soon as he saw his kind corrector after the business, he very gracefully and cordially thanked him, kissing his hand, with a bow, and saying, "Jack no more cry;" and as he really was hardly touched, and full well knew he

had not the heart to be severe, it was a proof of that openness
to rebuke which is a lovely mark of true Christianity.

Montgomery beautifully says,

> Prayer is the Christian's vital breath,
> The Christian's native air.

And so it eminently was with the dumb boy. Under every
form of condition and circumstance; in health and sickness; in
joy, in grief; in danger, in perplexity—over his food, his
studies, his work, his amusements, he was ever turning a look
of peculiar sweetness on me, with the two words, "Jack pray."
He always smiled when so engaged, and a look of inexpres-
sible eagerness, mingled with satisfaction, and the triumph of
one who feels he has taken a secure stand, told me when he
was praying, without any change of position, or looking up.
There was always a mixture of anxiety in his aspect when he
tried to make himself understood by his fellow-creatures; this
gave place to something the reverse of anxiety when he was
"talking to God," as he sometimes expressed it. He oftener
looked down than up; and very often did I see his eye fixed
upon the "Baby boy," when, as his looks bespoke, and as he
afterwards told me, he was "tell God" about him, and that he
was too little to know about Jesus Christ yet. Many a prayer
of that grateful dumb boy even now descends in blessings on
the head of my brother's "Baby;" and long may the hallowed
stream continue to flow down, until they rejoice together
before the throne of the Lamb!

One of Jack's lovely thoughts was this: he told me that
when little children began to walk, Jesus Christ held them by
the hand to teach them; and that if they fell, he put his hand
between their heads and the ground to prevent their being
hurt. Then, as if he saw this proceeding, he would look up,
and with the fondest expression say, "*Good* Jesus Christ! Jack
very much loves Jesus Christ." I hope you are not tired of Jack;
I have much to tell about him. God made me the humble
means of plucking this precious brand from the burning; and

I owe it to the Lord to show what a ten-fold blessing I reaped in it. Jack was not the only one of whom He has, in the dispensations of his providence, said to me, "Nurse this child for me, and I will give thee thy wages." I have found Him a noble Paymaster!

And now I come to a period of my life that I have scarcely courage to go over. Many, and sharp, and bitter were the trials left unrecorded here; and shame be to the hand that shall ever dare to lift up the veil that tender charity would cast over what was God's doing, let the instruments be what and who they might. It is enough to say, that even now I know that there was not one superfluous stroke of the rod, nor one drop of bitter that could have been spared from the wholesome cup. Besides, he dwelt most mercifully with me: those two rich blessings, health and cheerfulness, were never withdrawn. I had not a day's illness through years of tribulation: and though my spirits would now and then fail, it was but a momentary depression: light and buoyant, they soon danced on the crest of the wave that had for an instant engulphed them.

It is of joy that I have next to tell: safety, peace, prosperity, under the restored sunshine that had made my early career so bright. Never did a sister more fondly love a brother; never was a brother more formed to be the delight, the pride, the blessing of a sister. He was of most rare beauty from the cradle, increasing in loveliness as he grew up, and becoming the very model of a splendid man; very tall, large, commanding, with a face of perfect beauty, glowing, animated, mirthful—a gait so essentially military, that it was once remarked by an officer, "If Browne were disguised as a washerwoman, any soldier would give him the salute." He had also served in the Peninsula with the highest possible credit, regarded by those in command as one of the best officers in the service, and most ardently loved by the men under him. Many a bloody battle-field had he seen; but never did a wound reach him. On one occasion—Albuera—his gallant regiment went into action 800 strong, and on the following day only 96 men were able to draw rations. He became on the field a lieutenant, from being the youngest ensign; and alike in all circumstances he shone out as an honour to his profession. He had also been an especial favourite with John VI. of Portugal; and the high polish of a court was superadded to all the rest, without in the smallest degree changing the exceedingly playful, unaffected joyousness of the most sunshiny character I ever met with.

Ten years' absence had produced the effect on my sisterly love that Burns describes:—

> "Time, but th' impression stronger makes
> As streams that channels deeper wear."

I had also many personal reasons for looking forward to his return with peculiar anxiety: and its uncertainty increased the feeling. I had been spending a day with a sick friend, and ran home at night, to the lodging occupied by my mother and myself, and there I found my brother! What a dream those ten years' trial appeared!

We remained but a short time in Clifton, and soon bent our way towards the metropolis, where he expected, as is usual, to dance a long and wearisome attendance on the Horse-Guards, for a regimental appointment. He had refused that of aide-de-camp to King John, with any military rank and title that he might desire; preferring a half-pay unattached company of the British to any thing that a foreign service could offer; but he was mistaken: his merits were well known to the Duke of York, and before he could well state to Sir Herbert Taylor his wishes, that estimable man told him he had only to select out of two or three regiments lately returned from foreign service, and he would be gazetted on the following Tuesday. He chose the 75th, and was immediately appointed to it, with leave to study for two years in the senior department of the Military College at Sandhurst, the better to qualify himself for a future staff-appointment.

A sweet cottage, standing isolated on the verge of Bagshot Heath, sheltered by tall trees and opening on a beautiful lawn, with a distant but full view of the college, became our abode.

A delightful room was selected for me, with an injunction to sit down and make the most of my time while he was in the halls of study, that I might be at leisure to walk, to ride, to garden, to farm with him—my brother, my restored brother, whose eye beamed protection, and whose smiles diffused gladness, and whose society was what in our happy childhood it had ever been, just instead of all the world to me. If one thing was wanting, and wanting it was to knit us in a tie more endearing than any of this world's bonds could possibly be, that very sense of want furnished a stimulus to more importunate prayer on his behalf. Some of the good people who for lack of a relay of ideas borrow one of their neighbour's and ride it to death, treated me to a leaf from the book of Job's comforters, when the calamity fell on me of that precious brother's death, by telling me I had made an idol of him. It was equally false as foolish. An idol is something that either usurps God's place or withdraws our thoughts and devotions from him. The very reverse of this was my case: I had an additional motive for continually seeking the Lord, not only in prayer for the enlightening influences of the Holy Spirit on behalf of one so dear; but also for grace to walk most circumspectly myself, lest I should cast any stumbling-block in his way, or give him occasion to suspect that my religious profession was a name and not a reality. That was surely a profitable idol which kept me always prayerful before God, watchful over myself, diligent in the discharge of duties, and in continual thanksgiving for the mercies I had received! Do I repent loving my brother so well? I wish it had been possible to love him better. These warm affections of the heart are among the sweetest relics of a lost Eden, and I would sooner tear up the flowers that God has left to smile in our daily path through a sin-blighted wilderness—far sooner—than I would cease to cherish, to foster, to delight in, the brighter, sweeter flower of domestic love, carried to the full extent of all its endearing capabilities.

* * *

Hitherto many impediments had been thrown in the way of my literary labours. Anxiety, apprehensions, and the restlessness of feeling resulting from a continual change of abode, had broken the train of thought, and rendered my work very uncertain. Indeed, it would often have been wholly inadequate to my support, but for the watchful kindness of friends whom the Lord raised up to me, foremost among whom always stood the estimable Mr. Sandford, who never ceased to regard me with paternal affection and care. To be wholly independent was the first earthly wish of my heart; and now a fair opportunity was given of testing my willingness to labour diligently. The result was so far satisfactory, that in the course of the two years and two months of my residence under my brother's roof, I wrote The Rockite, The System, Izram, Consistency, Perseverance, Allan M'Leod, Zadoc, and upwards of thirty little books and tracts, besides contributions to periodicals. I was going on most prosperously, when an attempt was suddenly made from another quarter to establish a claim to the profits of my pen. The demand was, probably legal, according to the strict letter of existing statutes, though circumstances would have weighed strongly in my favour. But it greatly reduced the value of my copyrights, for the time being; and I found myself checked in my career at a juncture when it was especially my desire to go on steadily. This brought upon me two temptations, the force of which was greatly increased by the circumstances under which they found me.

LETTER XI.

SANDHURST.

When I first began to write, it was with a simple desire to instruct the poor in the blessed truths of the gospel: but my own situation soon rendered it needful to turn the little talent I possessed to account. This I did, still keeping in view the grand object of promoting God's glory; and my attempts having been well received, I found a ready market for whatever I wrote, so that the name was considered a sufficient guarantee for the book. Now, I could no longer safely use that name, and anonymous writing became the only feasible plan. A friend, who did not look upon the main subject in the light that I did, made, through my brother, a proposal that I should become a contributor to the most popular magazine of the day, supplying tales, &c. the purport of which was to be as moral as I pleased, but with no direct mention of religion. The terms offered were very high; the strict incognito to be preserved would secure me from any charge of inconsistency; and coming as it did when my regular source of income was suddenly closed, and when the idea of being burdensome to my generous brother with his increasing family was hardly supportable, it was thought I could not demur.

Nevertheless, I did; the Lord in his gracious providence had said to me, "Go, work to-day in my vineyard," and I had for upwards of four years enjoyed that blessed privilege. It was now withdrawn, certainly not without his permission, and how did I know that it was not to try my faith? The idea of hiring myself out to another master—to engage in the service

of that world, the friendship of which is enmity with God—
to cause the Holy One of Israel to cease from before those
whom by the pen I addressed,—to refrain from setting forth
Jesus Christ and Him crucified to a perishing world, and give
the reins to an imagination ever prone to wander after folly and
romance, but now subdued to a better rule—all this was so
contrary to my views of Christian principle, that after much
earnest prayer to God, I decided rather to work gratuitously
in the good cause, trusting to Him who knew all my necessity,
than to entangle myself with things on which I then could
not ask a blessing. The conflict was indeed severe; no one
attempted to oppose my resolve; but as yet no one could at
all understand its real ground, and it was a very trying position in which I stood, thus seemingly spurning an honourable
means of independence, and leaving myself destitute. But the
trial was short; my first friends, the "Dublin Tract Society,"
exercising that faith which has distinguished all their acts,
determined to brave the consequences, and still publish my
little books. This, though the profit was not then very good, I
hailed as a gracious intimation of the Lord's purpose still to
continue me in His service; and I was the more strengthened
to meet a second trial, which coming at a time when the sum
proffered would have been doubly acceptable, and the refusal
involving the loss of a very old and kind friend, was rather a
sharp one; more especially as the offence given would and did
alienate him from others who had no share in the proceeding,
and whose interests were far dearer to me than my own.

Many years before, that friend had published a novel; not
a flimsy love-story, but of a class above the common run. I
had, as a girl, been very fond of it, and often delighted the
amiable author by expressing an admiration that was not
general; for the work had failed, and was unsold. Now, finding
I had been myself successful with the pen, and full, even in
old age, of natural love for his literary offspring, he had
formed a plan in which he never dreamed of encountering
opposition. He wished me to re-write it, to cast the characters
anew, enliven the style, add variety to the incidents, and, in

short, make a new work out of his material. Still it was to be a novel; and as it had been originally published in his name, it was to be so now. My share in the work would never be known: and as he was abundantly wealthy, and equally generous, a *carte blanche* as to terms was before me.

On the former occasion I had paused, and thought much; on this I did not. The path was plain before me, but dreadfully painful to pursue. A hundred pounds, just then would have been more to me than a thousand at another time; and private feeling was most distressingly involved, both as regarded myself and others. It was in an agony of prayer, and after many bitter tears, that I brought myself to do what nevertheless, I had not a wish to leave undone. I wrote a faithful letter to the friend in question, most unequivocally stating the ground of my refusal—the responsibility under which I conceived we all lay before God for the application of talents committed by him; the evils of novel-reading; and, as far as I could, I declared the whole gospel of Christ to one whom I had no reason to regard as taking any thought whatever for his soul. I heard no more from him to the day of his death, which took place ten years after. I had reason to believe that his intentions towards me had been very liberal in the final distribution of his property; for he had known and loved me from my cradle, and he had no family: but my conscience bore a happy testimony in the matter; and I am fully persuaded that the whole was a snare of Satan to betray me into an acceptance of unhallowed gains, by catering to the worldly tastes of those who forget God. No doubt the business would have been a profitable one, and the inducement to persevere made strong in proportion as I sacrificed principle to lucre. "All these things will I give thee, if thou wilt fall down and worship me." I should neither do justice to the Lord's rich goodness, nor to the honoured instrument of His bounty, if I omitted to add, that, shortly after, my munificent friend Mr. Sandford sent me a gift that left me no loser by having done my duty.

While on the subject of my books, I will record an incident that occurred about the same time, and on which I always look with feeling of indescribable delight. I did not know it until, some years afterwards, the story was related to me by the principal actor in it—the abettor of my heretical pravity. Little did I dream, when writing my humble penny books, that they would be advanced to the high honour of a place in the Papal Index Expurgatorius!

The lady in question took to the continent a sweet, only daughter: a lovely little girl of only ten years old, the joy of her widowed bosom, who was fast sinking into decline. I was exceedingly fond of that child, who returned my affection from the depths of an Irish heart; and who, out of love for its author, selected one of my small penny books to translate into Italian during her last stage of suffering. She did not live to complete it: but with her dying breath requested her mother to do so, in the earnest hope of its being made useful to the ignorant people around them. Bessie was a lamb of the Lord's fold; and to lead other children into the same blessed shelter was her heart's desire. As soon as the bereaved mother could make any exertion, she betook herself to the task assigned to her departed darling, and found such satisfaction in it, that she extended her labours, and translated several more. Being a lady of rank and affluence, she was enabled to carry it on to publication, and to ensure the circulation of the little books among many. One of them, "The Simple Flower," a sixpenny-book, thus translated, fell into the hands of an Italian physician, a man of a highly-cultivated mind; nominally a Romanist; and like all thinking Romanists, in reality an infidel. The book contains not a word on controversy; not an allusion to Popery—it is plain gospel truth, conveyed in a very simple narrative. God blessed it to this gentleman, and he became a Christian. The circumstance excited much remark: curiosity led many to read that and others of the series, and a great number were circulated in the neighbouring districts. This was actually within the papal states, under the jurisdiction of the Archbishop of Sienna, to whose knowledge came the astounding fact that pennyworth's of heresy were circulated within the range of his pastoral charge. The matter was

reported at head-quarters; taken up with due seriousness, and
a Sunday appointed, on which, no doubt, I was quietly worshipping in the college-chapel at Sandhurst, wholly unconscious
that my name was then being proclaimed at a hundred Italian
altars, with a denunciation against all who should read,
circulate or possess any book, tract, or treatise, penned by me.
One instance was particularized: a poor priest had himself
given numbers of these translations to his flock; and after
mass he stood before them, deeply moved, telling them he
had a painful duty to perform. That he had received from the
highest authority a command to proclaim what he held in his
hand, and which he proceeded to read to them—a copy of
the fulmination above mentioned. Having done so, he folded
the paper and resumed, saying, he had given and recommended the little books to them, because he had read them
himself and found nothing but what was good in them:
however, the church, which they were all bound to obey,
judged otherwise; "and now," he added, "you must bring them
back to me, or burn them, or in some other way destroy them
wholly: nevertheless, I declare in the sight of God, I found no
evil in those dear little books, but the contrary—they are full
of good." He burst into tears, and many wept with him; and
not a few of the proscribed productions were wrapped up and
buried in the earth, or otherwise put away till the search should
be over. Who knows but that very priest was led to the Bible
and to Christ through such humble means? I would not
exchange for the value of the three kingdoms ten times
tripled, the joy that I feel in this high honour put upon me—
this rich blessing of being under the Papal curse.

I have been long silent on the subject of public events:
George the Third had passed into a blessed immortality just
at the time when I first learned to understand and appreciate
his Christian character. George the Fourth had visited Ireland,
and in the ardently expressed affection of a people who will
always love where they are permitted so to do, had recognized
their claim to his paternal regard; which recognition was used
by the wily deceivers of the day to press as a national boon

the wicked, cruel measure which would only confirm more strongly their subjection to a foreign power, and alienate the whole race from England. Napoleon had disappeared from the world of which he was the terrific scourge, and found an obscure tomb on the distant rock; while peace rested upon the nations, so long tossed in tumultuous rage. No sign appeared of hostile movement abroad, and all men were occupied in domestic politics, striving for and against the subversion of our ancient institutions. The party in power had shown a decided inclination to help forward the cause of Popery; and God, who has never failed to intimate his displeasure at such a leaning on the part of our government, shook the whole country with a commercial panic that menaced general bankruptcy. Alexander of Russia was taken away in the prime of life; and with full purpose of heart to christianize his vast empire, and to gather in the outcasts of Israel. I always thought he was removed because his enlightened mind was too far in advance of the time, and he pressed too rapidly forward in works not yet to be accomplished. His death affected me deeply, for I had become exceeding watchful of the signs of the times, and impressed with the belief that the consummation of all things was not far distant. In fact, I was rapidly embracing the views called Millennarian, without being conscious of it; and the prophetic Scriptures became unceasingly my study. The Duke of York's death seemed to be the signal for overthrowing our national Protestantism; and while I mourned in him a royal patron who had taken a general interest in my concerns, and in heartfelt sympathy wept with the old soldiers of the military establishment, over one so justly endeared to them and to the whole army, my heart quaked at the silencing of that voice so nobly, so energetically, so solemnly raised in the Senate against a deed to which he then distinctly vowed, before God and his country, that he would never be consenting. I visited St. George's chapel on the day of his interment; and when I saw his knightly effigies—the helm and sword and banner—taken down from over his stall, and carried out of the chapel, a strange foreboding came over me, such as I had never known; but which, alas! has long been and still is in course of fulfilment. I stood at the mouth of the vault where the relics of his royal father rested, and into which his own were to descend: it seemed to me the open grave of all that my proudly English heart had cherished from infancy: and such was my emotion that I declined witnessing the interment, and stationed myself in the highest attic of a house where all were thronging to the lower windows, for a sight of the solemn pageant that wound its torch-lit way through the street. I saw it far beneath me, more like a procession of fairies than of full-sized men and noble steeds: and I wept unrestrained, with feelings hard to define, until wholly exhausted, and actually ill from the effects of such excitement. Was there not a cause? The event has proved it. I cannot believe that the deed committed two years after-wards in that very Windsor, the granting of the royal assent to the abominable Bill, would ever have been perpetrated while the Duke of York existed as next in succession to the throne.

This was in January 1827: the following October witnessed the most eventful scene that has been enacted upon this globe for many centuries. Even at that time I felt it to be so; and now at the distance of thirteen years its effects are making themselves felt through every nerve and pulse of the body politic, not merely in Europe but gradually throughout the world. The battle of Navarino was the turning-point of this dispensation. Most wonderful it was in all its particulars: nothing could be further from the wishes, the interest, the avowed policy of England than to cripple in any way the power of Turkey, that great and efficient barrier against the formidable Muscovite. In fact our fleet was rather intended to protect than to embarrass the Porte. Greece was struggling for freedom, and the Mahommedan despot was crushing her deeper into the dust beneath his merciless hand, so that it behoved the civilized powers of Christian Europe to interpose something in the form of protection over the oppressed victim; but Russia alone had an interest in harming Turkey, and Russia's allies were of all things most jealous of her growing greatness: yet, unsent, unauthorized, and acting under an impulse that could not be accounted for, England and France went into action side by side with Russia, and at one blow broke for ever the power of the Porte. It was most wonderful: it opened to my view a mighty page in the world's history, and led me, without communication with any mortal holding those views—for I knew not one—to look upon the sixth vial as in the very act of emptying its contents on the great river Euphrates, and so to enquire, with trembling anxiety, what would be the result of the outpouring of the seventh. I settled it in my own mind to watch the east, as one who looks for the sun's rising on a scene of bodily peril, in darkness and in doubt. I plainly saw that Turkey must now lie helpless before the Russian; and I resolved, if this blow was not followed up by sudden ruin, but by the continuance of a wasting,—a "drying-up" process, I would proceed on my new assumption of prophetic meanings as established. Devoted to the Jewish cause, I always looked upon Turkey with abhorrence, and joyously anticipated her predicted subversion, that Israel might again possess the good land; and while shuddering over the scene of bloodshed that had occurred, and lamenting the passage of so many ruined souls into eternity, I could not stifle a sensation of joy that a signal-gun had thus been fired for the ingathering of the scattered tribes. My brother observed this: he said, "I do believe you are glad of this unfortunate battle; I promise you it is a very different victory from what you are used to exult in." I did not deny this, but still, in spite of myself, I looked glad. "Oh, you Christian ladies are tender-hearted creatures, to delight in a scene of butchering and drowning, just because the poor wretches happen to be Turks!" I could not defend myself from the charge: that dear brother had not yet learned to view passing events in the light that Scripture throws upon them: and I remained under a sort of stigma that did not affect me much: especially as his utmost displeasure never went further than good-humoured raillery, levelled at the supposed inconsistency which his own awakening perception of divine truth rendered him doubly quick at detecting. I was driven to my Bible more closely than ever by this event; and the Bible which had taught me every thing else, was now teaching me Millennarianism, while as yet the word was in my estimation one of reproach.

With what fondness does memory linger over those delighted days of sojourn under the sheltering roof of my brother, so soon to come to a final close, so far as this world was concerned. Another boy had been added to our happy little circle, and Jack's warm heart seemed to receive an accession of love, that he might have it to bestow on the "beautiful Baby small," which claimed so much of his thoughts and prayers. Indeed, his thoughts were always prayers, for God was in all. He made but little progress in language, having a great dislike to learning beyond what was needful for communicating his thoughts to me; and as he was obliged to be more with servants than I liked, I was not anxious to extend his facilities of communication with them: nor did he at all desire their society. He had a little room of his own, to his great delight, over the coach-house; and when not employed in his work, or talking with me, he was most happy with his pencil. He gave a strong and beautiful proof of the dread with which God inspired him as to ensnaring company; and I cannot pass it over.

My brother declared his intention of keeping a horse, and of course a groom. Jack came to me with an earnest entreaty that he might be the groom, saying he could do the duty well. The reason he gave to me, confidentially, was, that men were very wicked; that the man-servant would often shake hands with the devil (his usual mode of expressing wilful sin), and that if Jack shook hands with him, he would some day draw his hand till he got it into the devil's: meaning, that an evil companion would by degrees induce him to become evil too. He also said, Captain B. was very kind to Mam, and that a servant would cost him money, and eat a great deal; but Jack would take no money, and only eat "small potatoe, small meat," because he loved Captain B. When I communicated the request to my brother he laughed, saying, such a boy could never groom a horse; but Jack had been privately to a kind friend of his, a retired non-commissioned officer of cavalry, who had the care of some horses, and got him to give him instruction; succeeding so well in his attempt that the serjeant told my brother he really thought him competent to the office. He consented to try; and having purchased his horse, tied him up at the stable-door for Jack to commence operations, while we all assembled to see him. I was apprehensive of a total failure, but he did it admirably, and my brother declared he only wanted a few inches in height to be one of the best grooms in the kingdom. Jack's exultation was very great. When we were alone, he went up to the horse, kissed it and after telling me how pleased he saw his master look, he added, "No man! all one Jack. Devil cry—go devil!" and snapped his fingers at the invisible enemy. His greatest security next to his love of God was his constant fear of Satan; yet it was rather a fear of himself, lest he should yield to his temptations, for he was perfectly aware Satan could not force him to do anything. Hence his extreme caution as to what associates he had, and a reserve with those whom he did not know to be Christians, which was sometimes mistaken for pride. He invariably asked me, of every person who came to the house, whether that person loved Jesus Christ; and if I could not give a positive answer in the affirmative, he stood aloof; always most courteous, but perfectly cold, and even dignified in repelling any advance to sociability beyond common politeness. He did not know the meaning of a single bad word, and God kept him so that the wicked one touched him not. I used every means, of course, to this end. I watched him most narrowly, and always interposed if he was required to do anything, or to go to any place, in which I apprehended danger. My vigilance extorted smiles from those who considered it must be all in vain when he grew a little older, but no obstacle was placed in my way; and I blessed God I never relaxed that care, nor did the boy ever depart from his holy caution; and he died at the age of nineteen, a very tall and finelooking young man, with the mind of a little babe as regards the evil that is in the world. Oh that parents knew the importance of thus watching over their boys!

Soon after the first horse was established in his stall, my brother purchased a second for my riding, saying he should now of course get an assistant in the stable; but Jack burst into tears, and himself pleaded with him for leave to do all. My brother greatly delighted in his broken language, and caught exactly his phraseology, so that they conversed together as well as with me; and he told me he could not stand Jack's entreaties. "He is a fine little fellow," said he, "and if you will watch and see that he is not over-exerting himself, he may try for a while: he will soon be tired." But far from it; Jack was proud of his two horses: and none in the place were better kept. When a cow was added, a young person came to milk her; but Jack was outrageous, talked of his mother's "Kilkenny cows," and "Cow's baby," and expressed such sovereign contempt for the stranger's performance, and such downright hostility against the intruder, that we had no peace till he got the cow also under his especial care. Often afterwards did he talk of that time, saying he was "Well Jack" when he had two horses and a cow; and almost crying over his loss. He grew rapidly, and the doctors told me that such a life would have kept him strong to any age.

One day he came and asked me to let him have a large hoop, to make him go faster on messages. I thought it childish, and did not regard it, so he went to my brother with the same request, who inquired his reason. Jack told him the stage coaches that passed our gate went very fast, because the four horses had four large hoops, meaning the wheels, and if he had a large hoop he could go as fast as the horses. Diverted beyond measure at such an original idea, my brother sent to Reading for the largest and best hoop that could be got; and many a laugh we had at seeing Jack racing beside the London coaches, with his wheel, nodding defiance at the horses, and shouting aloud with glee. He often went six miles with his wheel, to bear messages and notes to our valued and much-loved friend, General Orde, whom he idolized almost, and who looked on him as one of the most lovely instances of divine grace he had ever met with. On the first formation of the British Reformation Society, General Orde wrote to me, with a prospectus of the intended work. I told it to Jack, who, in rapturous delight gave me his whole worldly fortune of two shillings, bidding me give it to put in their pockets, and to bid good General Orde tell gentlemen to send much Bibles to Kilkenny, that his father and mother and all the poor people might learn to break their crucifixes, and love Jesus Christ. I wrote this to the General, who sent to me for the identical two shillings, which Mr. Noel produced on the platform, with the dumb boy's message, and I believe it drew many a piece of gold from the purses of those who saw the gift, which stands enrolled the very first in the accounts of that noble society's receipts. Jack often prayed for the Reformation Society, and I believe his blessing helped them not a little. There was so much faith in all that he did, such as God alone could give; and he never seemed to entertain a doubt of obtaining what he asked. Many a sweet instance of his child-like confidence in the Lord is engraven on my memory, at once to stimulate and to shame me. His whole experience seemed to be an illustration of the word of promise, "Ask, and ye shall receive." One of the things that struck me as being referable to nothing but the teaching of the Holy Spirit, was the interest manifested by this boy for the Jews. His active Protestantism was easily accounted for: but to give him any idea of Judaism would have been impossible. He could not read. His knowledge of language did not go far enough to enable him to understand the construction of a sentence; and though he spelled correctly, and wrote readily whatever he wished to say, and his mode of expression was generally quite intelligible to others, he did not comprehend what was spoken or written in the ordinary way. Accustomed to attach a distinct meaning to every word, and acquainted with very few besides nouns and a few verbs, which he only used in the present tense, independent of the pronouns, and without reference to number, he was quite lost among the other parts of speech.

For instance, if I had wanted to say, "You must go to the village, and buy me a small loaf of bread," I should have expressed it thus: "Jack go village, money, bread small, one." Grammatically expressed, the order would have been unintelligible to him; but few would have misunderstood it in the uncouth phrase last instanced. He would have gone to the shop, and writing down, "Bread small, one," would have held out the money, and made a sign to express what size he wanted. It was this very fact of the impossibility of conveying to his mind any clear notion of things invisible and spiritual, that so gloriously manifested the power and goodness of God in causing the light to shine into his heart. To a reader who never witnessed the attempts of an intelligent, half-taught deaf mute, to express his meaning, and to catch that of others, much of what I state respecting Jack may and must appear, if not incredible, at least unintelligible; yet none who ever saw and conversed with him would fail to substantiate it, and they were very many. That zealous missionary, Dr. Wolff, visited my brother's cottage when he and I were both absent, and no one could assist Jack in conversing with him; yet so great was his delight that he wanted to take him to Palestine, to instruct the deaf and dumb in the doctrine of Christ. The Rev. H. H. Beamish is another who cannot without emotion recall his intercourse with that dying Christian. General Orde, who saw him very frequently, regarded him as a wonder of divine grace; and the Rev. W. Hancock, his beloved pastor, who for four years observed him closely, often said he derived greater encouragement from the experience and the prayers of that poor boy than from almost any earthly source. Unbelievers will doubt; but those who know the grace of our Lord Jesus Christ will adore.

Still it will be evident that Jack could not read the Bible. He took great delight in copying it out, dwelling on such words as he knew; but I have seen him turn over two leaves and go on, wholly unconscious of any mistake; and I have found among his papers whole pages, composed of half sentences, and single epithets from Scripture, put together in unbroken paragraphs, without any meaning. With all this he was ardently attached to the Jewish cause, and always told me "Jesus Christ love poor Jew: Jew soon see love Jesus Christ." When speaking of them, he would look very tender and sorrowful, moving his head slowly from side to side, and his hand as if stroking some object in a caressing way. At such times it was curious to mark the effect of naming a "priest Roman" to him. In a moment his aspect changed to something ludicrously repulsive; he stuck his hands in his sides, puffed out his cheeks to their full extent, scowled till his brows overhung his eyelids, and generally finished by appearing to seize a goblet and drain off the contents to the last drop, inflating his body, stroking it, smacking his lips, and strutting about. This he did, not as imputing drunkenness to the priesthood, but their denying the cup to the laity, and swallowing the contents themselves. Though his acting was laughably comic, his feeling was that of serious and severe indignation; and he would reprove us for the laughter it was utterly impossible to restrain, saying with, triumphant confidence, "God see, Jesus Christ come soon!" This coming of the Lord Jesus, an actual, personal, visible coming, to walk about on the earth, in whatever way he had represented it to himself, or howsoever God had revealed it to him, he constantly associated with two things— the consolation of the Jews and the destruction of Popery. I did not see it so; I looked for both these events at the commencement of the thousand years, expecting a spiritual coming of the Lord then, and a personal one at the very end of the world. I did not, however, contradict Jack, nor attempt to alter his views on the subject. I wanted the world to be quietly converted, by the preaching of the gospel; but I had once been nearly startled out of my system, when in Kilkenny. A beloved friend, since gone to her rest, pointed out to me the sixty-third of Isaiah, asking what I thought was the dye of the garments there mentioned! I replied, the blood of the Saviour which drenched his raiment in the garden, and his body on the cross. "And what," pursued she, "is this treading of the winepress?" I answered, "It was the laborious work of achieving our redemption, and bearing alone the wrath of the Lord." "I wish you would read it without a break," said she, "and take it according to the literal, plain sense, for I think we are all wrong here." I did read it, was surprised, and, contrary to my usual custom, ran to a commentary, and Matthew Henry's very lame and laboured elucidation, or rather extinction of the matter, checked the inquiry thus begun. On all other points I speedily came to a right understanding, because I took God's word as my guide; and only on this did I prefer a candle to the sun, just because Matthew Henry lay beside me, having been sent in by a friend. On this subject, therefore I remained in the dark, until the amazing turn of events in the East, put me upon considering the prophecies of the last days in the same way as I had considered all the other vital questions; and the result was, a reception of almost every millennial view before I suspected it, and before I ceased to abjure the name as wholly inconsistent with spiritual Christianity.

*   *   *

LETTER XII.

SEPARATION.

The two shortest years of my life were now drawing to a close. My brother had completed his studies, passed his examination, and was under orders to join his regiment in Ireland. Oh how my heart rose in prayer, that where I had found a spiritual blessing, he might also receive it! I could not understand the state of his mind on the most vital of all points; he had imbibed a prejudice so strong against the class of people called evangelical, that nothing but his generous affection for us would have induced him to receive under his roof two of that proscribed body—to say nothing of Jack. He confessed to me, laughing, not long after we became its inmates, that he had supposed we should be falling on our knees half a dozen times a day, singing psalms all over the house, and setting our faces against everything merry or cheerful. He had never been acquainted with any serious person before going to Portugal, nor during his short leaves of absence at home: none of that class ever crossed his path abroad, and he came home prepared to believe anything that was told him of the supposed fanatics; whom he understood to be a sort of ranting dissenters. At Clifton, extremes then ran far; the gay people most violently denouncing their sober neighbours, and making up all sorts of scandal concerning them. Hannah More was pointed out as "queen of the Methodists," and a most infamous lie, wholly destructive of her moral character, circulated among a narrow but dissipated clique as a known fact; while the small fry of fanatics were disposed of by dozens in a similar way. The faithful clergyman whose ministry we attended was absolutely persecuted; and his congregation could expect no better at the same hands. I am very far from charging this upon the generality of even worldly people there; but it did exist, visibly and sensibly; and my dear brother evidently had fallen in with some of these wholesale calumniators, before he could possibly judge for himself. A visit to Barley Wood, and a very prolonged interview with the "queen" greatly staggered his prejudices; he was perfectly charmed with her, and remarked to me that if all her subjects were like her, they must be a very agreeable set of people. Still he apprehended an outbreak of extravagance when we should be fairly installed in his abode; and though he soon became undeceived, and learned to take the greatest delight in the society of General Orde, Mr. Sandford, and others equally decided—though he punctually attended the faithful ministry of Mr. Hancock at the college-chapel, besides his regular appearance at the usual military service, and would not allow one disparaging word to be uttered in his presence of that zealous preacher or his deeply spiritual discourses; though he chose from among his brother officers a bold, uncompromising Christian as his most intimate associate, and gave many unconscious indications that he had received the doctrine of man's total corruption, and the nothingness of his best works; though he became the warm advocate of a scriptural education for the youthful poor, whom he had always before considered most safe and happy in total ignorance—still, with all this, I could not see even in his beautifully devout bearing in public worship where the reverse so sadly prevailed, and where everything approaching to seriousness became a matter of suspicion, that he was really seeking God. In fact, I had been too much in the trammels of a system, which lays down arbitrary rules, and will not admit that God is working, unless his hand be immediately and openly apparent to all. I would not believe that what looked green and beautiful was a blade of corn, just because it had not yet grown to an ear: and I refrained from speaking, when perhaps speech on such subjects would have been more welcome than he wished to acknowledge, lest the remarks that I longed to utter might prove unpalatable, and produce the contrary effect to what I desired. He was only going for a little while: an appointment on the home staff was promised, and then I was to live with him again, and I would zealously pursue the work. Alas! what a rod was prepared for my unbelief and presumption! The present was slighted, in the confident expectation of a future that was never to arrive.

We were almost always together, out of his college hours. My window commanded a view of the distant building, and when I saw the preparatory movement to breaking up, I rose from my desk, tied on my bonnet, and ran off in sufficient time to meet him very near the college. Both let loose from six hours' hard work, we were like children out of school, often racing and laughing with all the buoyancy of our natural high spirits. The garden, the poultry-yard, and all the little minutiæ of our nice farming establishment, fully occupied the afternoon; while the children gambolled round, and Jack looked on with all smiles, often telling me how much he loved "beautiful Capt. B——" as he constantly called him. At ten o'clock we parted for the night, I to resume the pen till long after midnight; he to rest, whence he always rose at four o'clock, devoting four or five hours to study before we met in the morning. We visited very little, domestic retirement being the free choice of every one of us; and nothing could have induced my brother to banish his children from the parlour or drawing-room. Few things excited his indignation more than the nursery system; his little ones were the pride of his heart, the delight of his eyes, the objects of his fondest care. He often said he intended his boys to be gentlemen, and therefore would not allow them to imbibe the tastes and habits of the kitchen. The consequence is that his boys *are* gentlemen.

Thus dwelling in love, united in every plan and pursuit, our time fairly divided between diligent work and healthful recreation, amid the delights of rural life, do you marvel that I call this period my two shortest years! Had no previous circumstances given ten-fold brilliancy to these lights by casting a depth of black shadow behind them, or no menacing future hung over the present enjoyment, still there was enough to make it indeed an oasis: but it was more. I cannot doubt that the Lord mercifully gave me a foreboding of what was to come, in the intolerable anguish of what seemed to be but a very short parting, with a delightful prospect of renewed domestic comfort just beyond. Yet so it was: I almost died under the trial of that farewell; and for three weeks before, and as long after, I never had a night's rest. Visions of terror were constantly before me, among which a scene of drowning was so perpetually recurring that I have often started from my bed under the vivid impression. This was the more strange because we had always been so fearlessly fond of the water; in our early days we had a little boat, just big enough for him to row and me to steer, in which we used to take excursions on the river Wensum, and never thought of danger. At Sandhurst too we were frequently upon the lake, and had both become familiarized with ocean, until of all perils those of the water were least likely to daunt me, either for myself or him: yet in most imminent peril we had once been placed; and at this time it would recur to my memory with tormenting frequency.

I was about seven years old, and he, though younger, was much the larger of the two, a stout hearty boy, and I a very frail delicate little creature, thanks to the doctors and their pet drug. Our parents went out for a day's excursion, with a friend, and of course we accompanied them. The place was one celebrated for good fishing, and the gentlemen having enjoyed a long morning's sport, remained in the house with my mother, sending us out to play. We had a strict charge not to go too near the water, nor on any account to get into a boat, of which there were several on the river. We strolled about, and at last came to the brink of this river, to admire a large barge or wherry which lay close to the little pier; for it was a public ferry, and the depth very great. A small boat just by attracted my brother's attention, who wished to get into it, until I reminded him of the prohibition; when he said, "I wont get into it, Cha.: but I will sit down here and put my two feet in the little boat." He did so; the boat moved, and in his alarm, trying to rise, he fell and disappeared.

I perfectly remember the scene; I have also heard it described many a time by others, but I cannot understand how it was that I, stooping from the shore, with nothing to hold on by way of support, seized the little fellow by the collar as he rose, and firmly held him in my grasp. He did not struggle, but looked up in my face, and I down in his, and as I felt my puny strength rapidly failing, the resolution was firm on my mind to be drawn in and perish with him. There was not a question about it; I can recall the very thought, as though it was of yesterday; and I am positively certain that I should have tightened my hold in proportion as the case became more desperate. It pleased God that, just then, some men returning from work descried the figure of a little child stooping in a most dangerous position over the deep water: they ran up, and while one held me the others rescued the boy. My grasp was not unloosed until they had him safe on shore; he was then insensible, and I lost every recollection until I found myself still in the arms of the man who had carried me in, while my mother and the rest were stripping the rescued boy and chafing his limbs before a fire. It was much talked of, and many a caress I got for what they considered heroism beyond my years; but what heroism is like love? "Many waters cannot quench love, neither can the floods drown it; if a man would give all the substance of his house for love, it would utterly be contemned."

When my brother departed for Ireland we left that sweet cottage and went to reside in the village, in one better suited to the size of our diminished family party. I had several young friends among the cadets, in whom I took a warm interest, and whose occasional visits I endeavoured to make as profitable to them as might be. It is a sad thing to see a boy, perhaps most carefully brought up by tender, and even Christian parents, watched, and kept as far as possible from all evil communication, then thrown at once into a large public institution, and exposed to every danger that can assail the youthful mind. A little insight into human nature must show any candid person the extent of mischief to be expected. Rarely do we find a case of conversion, with establishment in grace, very early in life; and where it exists as remarkably as in Jack, we may learn from his excessive dread of exposure to temptation how vigilantly the young plant should be guarded. Let us just suppose, what is indeed no stretch of imagination, but a slight sketch of acknowledged reality—let us suppose a boy at the age when they are eligible for these places, acquainted with the truth, accustomed to Christian instruction, taught to look into the word of God for daily direction, and to seek in prayer the daily supply of needful grace; consider him as having remained under the eye of Christian parents, or of a schoolmaster who regards those committed to his care as immortal beings, for whose well-doing while under his charge, he is responsible to God; and who therefore counsels them well, and banishes to the utmost of his power, vice and profaneness from among them; affording them the usual domestic means of grace, and seeing that they are not neglected. Thus prepared, the lad enters upon a new scene, where he finds himself surrounded by a large number of youthful companions, all busy in qualifying themselves for a future career, we will say in the service of their country. The first thing done is to try the metal of the new comer, by putting upon him some insult, which if he resents, offering to fight his way, he may be looked on with due respect; but if he appears timid, or reluctant to retaliate, he may be assured of becoming the object of a most harassing persecution, for the amusement of the thoughtless, and the gratification of the cruel. In either case, he passes an ordeal of great severity particularly during the night, when nothing is deemed too rough or alarming for the poor stranger to encounter. I appeal to those who have passed it, whether this is not enough to turn the brain of a weak-minded youth, or to injure severely the body of a delicate one: I have myself known an instance, in a great public seminary, wherein derangement and death followed.

Supposing this well got over, the lad then finds that if there be any among his new comrades disposed to keep up the practice of reading the scriptures and prayer, they must do it as secretly as they would commit a murder, and find it more difficult to accomplish than any crime that could be named. There always will be a large proportion of ruffianly characters among many boys; some naturally so, others made so by examples. These have the ascendancy of course: and they will use it to check and to stifle whatever might shine in contrast to themselves; while, what with those unstable characters who will always row with the stream, and prudent ones who will not provoke hostility, and timid ones who dare not, they meet with little if any opposition, but rule the whole mass for evil.

*　　*　　*

Honourable men, after this world's course, who are themselves wholly in the dark, verily believing that religion would turn a youth's brain and unfit him for the active business of life, will feel it a part of their duty to oppose every possible obstacle to such attempts at reclaiming the young wanderers under their charge. I knew, and knew right well, an instance wherein a lady who strove to do good to the souls of some young lads whose parents she knew to be praying people, had a sort of ban put upon her, by the publication of an express order that they should not be again permitted to visit her: and when a nobleman who well knew that she had not done anything to merit such public condemnation, asked the Principal of the institution the reason for so harsh a proceeding, he received this answer, "My lord, I was sorry to do it: I felt it a painful duty, but an imperative one. The fact is, she got hold of some of the most promising lads under my care, and so infected them with her own gloomy notions, that, I give you my word, they were seen walking alone, with bibles in their hands." So much the wiser are the children of this world in guarding those committed to them from the entrance

of spiritual good, than are the children of light in protecting their dearest treasures from the contamination of most
deadly evil!

But to return to my cadets at Sandhurst. I had two young
friends there, both Irish, who were known to me from
childhood; both greatly attached to my brother; both loving
me dearly; and many a happy hour we passed, strolling over
the wild heath, or enjoying the cheerfulness of my cottage
home. On those two, among many, I looked with especial
solicitude as to their future course: and I have had to rejoice
in different ways, over them both. One was early taken to his
rest; he died in the faith, looking simply to the Lord Jesus, and
finding perfect peace in him. The other was long away on
foreign service, and when next I saw him it was as the
deliverer, under God, of a whole town, and probably through
that of the whole kingdom, from a scene of revolutionary
carnage. He commanded the gallant little body of troops at
Newport, who on the 4th of November, 1839, quelled the
Chartist insurrection, and broke the formidable power that
menaced a general outbreak. I cannot pass over this event, it
was so delightfully gratifying to me.

A third of those in whom I took a lively interest was
Alexander Count Calharez, the eldest son of the Duc de
Palmella. He was a most elegant youth, of fine mind, delicate
feelings, and the sweetest manners possible. Devotedly attached
to Romanism, he constantly attended mass at the house of the
old Abbé, who added to his professorship in the Royal
Military college the duties of a popish priest. It was a sore
grief to me to see Calharez pursuing his solitary way to that
house, while we took the road to the College chapel, and met
him half way. I longed to enter a solemn protest against his
delusion, but I never did it in direct terms, though very often
dwelling, in his presence, on the peculiar truths of Christianity,
opposed as they are to the lie in which he trusted. I hoped to
have enjoyed many future opportunities of conversing with
him, for he always sought our society in preference to many
things that appeared more attractive, and took a lively interest

in Jack. But the College did not suit his taste; he left it soon, and accompanied his father to Portugal. He died at the Azores; and I have been told that his hope at the last was one which maketh not ashamed. He was the subject of many prayers; the last day will tell whether they were answered.

But I must hasten through the heaviest part of my task; it is the rending open of a wound never to heal until the leaves of the tree of life shall be laid upon it; and if by any means I do attain to that resurrection *from among* the dead, in which none but the Lord's children shall partake, surely the dear object of all this sorrow will be there beside me!

Six months had passed from the time of his departure to Ireland, and all his letters were full of cheerfulness, and pleasant anticipation. On the subject where I most wished to know his feelings, he was silent; but a passage in one of his letters struck me greatly. I had been suffering from a slight local pain, which one of my medical friends erroneously pronounced to be a disease of the heart; and in communicating this to him I had noticed, that I must live in momentary expectation of sudden death. His reply was very affectionate. He said it had given him a great shock, but on a little reflection he was convinced of its being altogether a nervous sensation; adding, "If not, why should you shrink from sudden death? For my own part, I should desire it, as a short and easy passage out of this life." A tremor came over me as a read these words; but again I thought, "Surely there is some-thing on his mind to brighten that passage, or he would not so express himself;" and the thought of many perils surrounding him quickened me to redoubled prayer, that God would set his feet upon the Rock of Ages.

It was on a bright Sabbath morning, at the end of June, that, having rather overslept myself, I found, on awaking, the letters brought by early post lying on my pillow. I took one: it was the Horse-Guards envelope, in which his letters usually came; and in my eagerness to open one from him I did not even put up a prayer. Full of smiling anticipation, I unfolded the enclosure, which was from a most dear and valued friend at the Horse-guards; and after some tender preparation, which the sudden reeling of my terrified brain prevented my comprehending, came the paralyzing sequel. A letter had been received from Mullingar—he was on the lake fishing— the boat overset! I could not understand the meaning of the words; but I understood the thing itself. I sprang to my knees to cry for mercy on him—but, oh that dreadful, dreadful thought that pierced through my inmost soul—"He is beyond the reach of prayer!" I fell back as if really shot; but what avails it to dwell on this? I bore it as God enabled me; I felt crushed, annihilated as it were, under the fierce wrath of the Lord; for to aggravate the blow, I had no power to believe or to hope. It was a light thing to have lost him, my all in this cold, dreary world, who from early infancy, had been as the light to my eyes, and the life-blood to my heart; he who had so very lately been restored, as if to show, that while he remained, all I could desire of earthly happiness was within my reach; he who had been to me instead of every other mortal blessing, and to whom I looked for all that I dared hope of future comfort. It was a light thing to have lost him, and to look upon the anguish of his widowed mother, to whom he had ever been more of a ministering angel than a son, and upon the tears of his little daughter, who had lost a father indeed! All this was a small matter compared with the overwhelming horrors of that unbelieving thought, that *he* had lost his soul.

*   *   *

Many a one came about me, offering the affectionate consolation that they rightly judged would be most soothing to my wounded spirit—the assurance that he for whom I mourned was in heaven. They dwelt on the blamelessness of his life; the beauty of his character; his exemplary discharge of every relative duty; the bright example that he placed before his brother officers, in discouraging all profaneness and profligacy, and strictly attending upon every religious ordinance.

Even the circumstance of his marked non-conformity with the disgraceful but almost universal custom of sitting during prayer in the church, was not forgotten; nor the devoted kindness with which he invariably conveyed to me every word of the sermon. And when my sickened heart perhaps too plainly spoke in my countenance the reply, " Miserable comforters are ye all!" or when I distinctly told them that these things did not content me, great was their astonishment. Full well I knew that to be admitted into heaven, my lamented one must have been *in Jesus* before the summons came, and "that not by works of righteousness which he had done" could he be saved. I secretly caught at the hope, that these fruits, once profitless and vile from being borne on a wild tree, had become rich and precious through grafting into the good olive. In God's sight old things may pass away, and all things become new, where man detects little change. By such thoughts was I consoled during the weeks that intervened before I had ground given me for confident thanksgiving, on the score of evidence that the blessing I had so earnestly sought was indeed vouchsafed.

Meanwhile, what a tenfold recompense for all the care bestowed on him did I reap in the beautiful sympathy of the dumb boy. When I came down stairs that dreadful morning he met me with a face of such wild dismay as even then arrested my attention. He uttered an audible "Oh!" of most touching tone, and thus expressed the impossibility he felt of realizing the tidings: "Jack *what?* Jack asleep? Jack see no— think no. Jack afraid very. Beautiful Captain B. gone?—dead? *What?*" and he stamped with the impatience of that fearfully inquisitive *what.* I answered, "Captain B. gone: water kill, dead." Tears stole down his loving face as he responded, "Poor mam! Mam one" (meaning I was now alone in the world). "God see poor mam one; Jesus Christ love poor mam one." With a feeling of bitter agony I asked him, "What? Jesus Christ love Captain B.?" "Yes," he replied, after a moment's solemn thought on the question: "Yes, Jack much pray; mam much pray; Jesus Christ see much prays." This was true comfort; all the eloquence of all the pulpits in England could not have gone to my heart like that assurance, that Jesus Christ had *seen* his many dumb prayers on behalf of that lost—oh, I could not even in the depth of my unbelieving heart say "lost one." I again asked the boy, "Jack much pray?" He answered with solemn fervency, "Very, very much pray. Jack pray morning, pray night; Jack pray church, pray bed. Yes, Jack many days very pray God make;—and he finished by signs, that wings should be made to grow from my brother's shoulders, for him to fly to heaven, adding, *Jesus Christ must make the wings*; and then with a burst of delighted animation, he told me that he was a "very tall angel, very beautiful."

I have repeated this conversation to shew the broken language carried on between us; and also how powerfully he expressed his thoughts. Soon after, when I was nearly fainting, a glass of water was held to my lips. I am ashamed to say, I dashed it down, exclaiming, "that murderer!" Jack caught my eye, and echoing my feelings, said in a bitter way, "Bad water!" then with a look of exulting contempt at the remaining fluid, he added, "Soul gone water? No!" This idea, that the soul was not drowned, electrified me; so good is a word spoken in due season, however trite a truism that word may be.

That night I pretended to go to bed, that others might do so too; and then I left my room, went to my little study, which was hung round with Jack's sweet drawings, and sat down, resting my elbows on the table, my face on my hands, and so remained for a couple of hours. Day had scarcely broken brightly upon me, about two in the morning, when the door opened softly, and Jack entered, only partially dressed, his face deadly pale, and altogether looking most piteously wretched. He paused at the door, saying, "Jack asleep, no; Jack sick, head bad—no more see beautiful Captain B." I could only shake my head, and soon buried my face in my hands again. However, I still saw him through my fingers; and after lifting up his clasped hands, and eyes, in prayer for me, he proceeded to execute the purpose of his visit to that room. Softly, stealthily, he went round, mounting a chair, and unpinned from the wall every drawing that contained a ship, a boat, or water under any form of representation. Still peeping at me, hoping he was not observed, he completed this work, which nothing but a mind refined to the highest degree of delicate tenderness could ever have prompted, and then stopping at the door, cast over his shoulder such a look of desolate sorrow at me, that its very wretchedness poured balm into my heart. Oh what a heavenly lesson is that, "Weep with them that do weep," and how we fly in its face when going to the mourner with our inhuman, cold-blooded exhortations to leave off grieving! Even Job's tormenting friends gave him seven days' true consolation, while they sat silent on the earth, weeping with him.

But God put into the dumb boy's heart another mode of consolation, which I must recount, as a specimen of his exceedingly original and beautiful train of thought. He used to tell his ideas to me as if they were things that he had seen: and now he had a tale to relate, the day after this, which rivetted my attention. He told me my brother went on the lake in a little boat, and while he was going along, the devil got under it, seized one side, pulled it over, and caught my brother, drawing him down to the bottom, which, as he told me, was deep, deep; and flames under it. Then Jesus Christ put his arm out of a cloud, reached into the water, took the soul out of the body, and drew it into the sky. When the devil saw the soul had escaped, he let the body go, and dived away, crying, Jack said, with rage, while the men took it to land. The soul, he continued, went up, up, up: it was bright, and brighter, "like sun—all light, beautiful light." At last he saw a gate, and inside many angels, looking out at him: but two very small angels came running to meet the soul; and when he saw them, he took them up in his arms, kissed them, and carried them on towards the gate, still kissing and caressing them. I was amazed and utterly at a loss, and said, "Two angels? What? Mam not know—what?" He looked at me with a laugh of wonder; pointed to my head and the wooden table, and replied (his usual way of calling me stupid,) "Doll Mam! Two small boys, dead, Portugal." My brother had lost two babes in Portugal; and thus exquisitely, thus in all the beauty of true sublimity, had the untaught deaf and dumb boy pictured the welcome they had given their father on approaching the gate of heaven.

A day or two after, some kind sympathizing relations and friends being assembled at the dinner-table, something cheerful was said, which excited a general smile. Jack was in the act of handing a plate he looked round him with a face of stern indignation, set down the plate, said "Bad laughing!" and walked out of the room, stopping at the door to add to me, "Mam come: no laughing; Gone—dead." I had not smiled; and this jealous tenaciousness of such a grief, on the part of an exceedingly cheerful boy, was the means of soothing more than any other means could have done it, the anguish of that wound which had pierced my very heart's core. These were a small part of the munificent wages that my Master gave me for nursing a child of His.

My first act had, of course, been to adopt my brother's son—the "Baby-boy"—now five years old, who had been, since he first showed his little round face in England, my own peculiar treasure. I begged him, as a precious boon, and for his sake bore up against the storm of sorrow that was rending me within. Jack fell into a decline, through the depression of his spirits in seeing me suffer; for to conceal it from one who read every turn of my countenance was impossible: and I should have been well content to sink also, but for the powerful motive set before me. Under God who gave him to me, you may thank your young friend for what little service I may have rendered in the cause you love, since 1828: for the prospect which by the Lord's rich mercy is so far realized, of seeing him grow up a useful honourable member of society, with right principles grounded on a scriptural education, was what enabled me to persevere, against every difficulty and every discouragement that could cross my path. I set up a joyful Ebenezer here; and I ask your prayers that the blessing may be prolonged, increased, perfected, even to the day when we shall all meet before the throne of God.

LETTER XIII.

NATIONAL APOSTACY.

Eighteen hundred and twenty-nine arrived. Most hateful year in the annals of England's perfidy to her bounteous Lord! I was never really roused from the lassitude of spirits that my loss had occasioned, until the conviction that the sin was about to be perpetrated forced itself on me: and a fervent desire to be found among those who were *actively* dissentient from it overcame all the langour consequent upon such a season of bitter affliction. For, what was it that England was about to do?

The Gospel had been preached here in the very early days of Christianity, probably by an apostle; and an independent church, small indeed but scriptural, existed; sufficient to offer serious opposition to the Romish delegate, Augustine, when he was deputed to incorporate this country in the growing mass of papal dependencies. The struggle was not of long duration; Rome, not then arrived at the full stature of the Apocalyptic Beast, prevailed: more by the lances of despotic monarchs than through the willing assent of Britons, either lay or ecclesiastical. Once subjugated, England lay at the foot of the Popes, from generation to generation, with now and then a movement towards freedom, which was soon stilled again by the iron sceptre: or perhaps I should rather say by a rap on the head with the iron key. In the time of Richard II. blood shed openly for the truth's sake began to give testimony that martyrdom would yet become the order of the day here; the spirit of persecution waxed bolder and fiercer, as the voice of scriptural protestation was heard: and the temporary check given to Roman usurpation by the decided proceeding of Henry VIII. in casting off the Pope's supremacy for his own private benefit, was followed by the blessed interval of young Edward's reign; during which God was, for the first time since foreign delegates got footing here, acknowledged and worshipped according to the Scriptures. Then had the church peace, and the land prosperity.

Mary followed: she ravened like a she-wolf in innocent blood. Popery ruled supreme; and the consequence was that the three years and a half of its domination may be characterized as one continuous act of murder. Then came Elizabeth, who, though she did not sufficiently purge out the old leaven, yet as she established Protestant ascendancy on a strong basis, exalted her kingdom to a height never before known: and James I. treading in the same steps, found his reign equally prosperous. Charles I. attempted to give preponderance to the evil again: and in that attempt brought upon his people a fearful civil war, and upon his own head an ignominious death. Charles II. worked covertly, under the service of a profligacy almost equalling that of Rome itself, to bring back upon our fathers the yoke of that odious bondage; and James II. set about the same enterprise openly. Then it was that, to avert another era of blood and flame, our ancestors removed from the throne the perverse line of Stuart, and placed upon it a devoted Protestant prince; restricting the succession to those heirs alone who should hold and solemnly swear to maintain the religion of the Bible, against all future attempts of the Western Antichrist to recover his lost footing among us.

From time to time, as fresh treasons rendered them necessary, restrictions were also laid on the legislative and corporative elections; until in all its parts the body politic of England presented a pure image of Protestantism, undefiled by the Babylonish garment or wedge of polluted gold: and while we thus acknowledged God openly, he openly acknowledged us. No weapon formed against England prospered;

she proved, as a nation, that she could not bear them which were evil; she had tried them that said they were apostles and were not, and had found them liars, and cast them out. For this cause, the Lord made her mountain to stand strong: Protestant England was everywhere invincible. Abroad victorious over every foe; at home, enabled to crush every attempt at insurrection. A little insulated spot on the world's map, she was as the city of David, alike the repository and the fortress of God's pure faith. How could I, with the Bible before me, cast a glance over the history of England, and question for one moment that my country's strength lay in her PROTEST?

And if patriotism had been as alien to my heart as it was paramount there, still allegiance to my God demanded that I should not see Him robbed, and the spoil given to his most presumptuous foe without an effort to free my own soul from any possible implication in the deed. "What had a woman to do with the proceedings of senators and governors?" Much. Everything. Was it a small matter that I enjoyed personal safety, personal liberty, and the free use of the Bible? Why was the hand of violence restrained from taking my life, under such sanction as that which blessed the butchers of Wexfordbridge in their work of slaughter? Why were no convent-walls ready to immure me; no dungeons sealed from public scrutiny by a power that might trample on the neck of secular law? Why had I not been taught in early life that a fellow-mortal held in his hands the power of saving or destroying my soul, and then commanded by that irresistible authority to abstain from looking into the word of God? Because I was the subject of a Protestant country, basking in the sunshine of its spiritual light, and sheltered by the enactments of a state that owned no earthly power superior to its own. It is true I might expect that in the course of my natural life the small beginnings of apostacy should grow to such fullness as to interfere with my own privileges: but was such base selfishness to harden my heart against a succeeding generation? Was I to contemplate the probability that the little fellow resting on my knee would be exposed to all from which I naturally shrunk?

Nor did I at all question the probability of a more rapid desolation than human wisdom could calculate on. Apostacy is so peculiarly a sin against God, such a dire provocation of His vengeance, that it might be expected that if we so walked contrary to him he would not wait till we, in the regular process of a rebellious march, brought ourselves within the range of his consuming fire, but that He also would walk contrary to us, with rage and with fury, and chastise us yet seven times more for our sins. Looking at the present fearfully-advanced stage of our revolt, and the perils that hem us in, all traceable to that fatal act, I can truly say that I was prepared for such a rapid motion, if once we began to descend the hill. View it as I would, the sinfulness of the proceeding by which we were voluntarily to renew the ancient alliance with Antichrist, and to give the priests of Baal authority to legislate for the ordering of God's temple, and invite anew the dangers, both spiritual and temporal, from which our fathers had been almost miraculously delivered, was too palpable for a moment's hesitation. I have said the priesthood would have power to legislate for us; and so they have at this moment. Every layman of that communion is the mere puppet of his priest; he receives directions how to act; and he must declare in confession, whether he has obeyed those directions to the letter. The Romish priests sit in parliament more effectually than if they took their places on the benches there: and each separate priest is simply and solely the active delegate of a foreign power, which uses the whole machinery for one work, to one end, and counts nothing advantageous that does not afford a distinct step towards the regaining of a despotic rule over this kingdom.

"But suppose a woman feels herself called on to take a personal interest in public affairs, what can she do, without stepping out of her proper sphere, and intruding into the province of the superior sex?" I am going to tell you what a woman may do; for of us it may be surely said, "Where there's a will there's a way." When we set our hearts upon any thing, we are tolerably enterprizing and persevering too, in its attainment;

and this natural love of pleasing ourselves may be turned to a very good account. No one grieves more than I do when a cowardly Barak shrinks from marching forward without female countenance and guidance; but the cause of God and his Church must not be placed in jeopardy through the pusillanimity of a thousand Baraks.

The first thing I did was to introduce a separate supplication into our family devotions morning and night, that God would avert the sin from this country: and twice a week I called on my neighbours, as many as would come, to join in express prayer to the same effect. I then inquired how the public mind at Sandhurst stood affected, and found the ruling powers, civil, military, and ecclesiastical, all going most complacently with the stream, while their views, of course, influenced many around them. Among the tradespeople and labouring classes, I saw that the subject had never occupied their thoughts, nor did they regard it as a matter at all concerning them. Indeed, in this lay the secret of the enemy's success: a vast body of Englishmen, who would have sprang forward in uncompromising hostility against any known invasion of their dearest birthright, were kept profoundly ignorant that such outrage was in contemplation. The other party were glad to leave them so; and on our side there was a grievous lack of effort in acquainting our poor neighbours with the danger impending over *their* temporal and spiritual blessings no less than our own. I procured a large number of simple tracts, explaining, on scriptural grounds, the dreadful nature of Popery, and the sinfulness, no less than the peril, of taking such an inveterate foe to our bosoms. These I ordered to be left at the cottages and shops for some way round, that the people might examine, and judge for themselves.

The Rector of the parish I knew very well: he was a very clever man, much devoted to literature, and in his politics wholly opposed to the measure; but alike averse from any personal exertion, and from drawing down on himself the censures of his more liberalized neighbours. He had been to Oxford, to vote against Peel, solely on the ground of his defection from the Protestant cause; and most heartily, though quite inactively, desired the defeat of the Emancipators. I represented to him the importance of doing what he could to accomplish his own wishes: he replied, he did not think there were nineteen men in the parish who cared enough about it to sign a petition, and he was unable to explain it to them all: but if I thought I could get that number of names (the *minimum* for a parochial petition, I believe,) and would write such an address to the King and the two Houses as he could approve, he would adopt it, sign his name, and in fact be very glad of my success. I went home, sent off to Staines for some pretty large skins of parchment, and wrote the petitions in terms as temperate, as concise, and as uncompromising as I could command. The Rector was greatly pleased; signed with much alacrity; and requested the churchwardens to do the same officially, as they were quite of our mind: this being done, I had before me the task of procuring nineteen signatures within two days.

I did not even go to a single individual myself: next door to me resided a townsman of my own, a schoolmaster, who held the old principles dear as his very life; he was secretly lamenting the coming evil, without a hope of being permitted in any way to oppose it; and you may believe with what delight he responded to my call, when asked to assist me. He went round to those who had previously received the little tracts, and to some of the small hamlets, or clusters of cottages scattered throughout the parish. He strictly adhered to my injunction to admit no signature of any youth under seventeen years; nor of any who did not seem to understand what they were doing, and why. I scattered the tracts and handbills as widely as I could; asked several intelligent men of an humble class to speak of it among their acquaintance; and at the end of the second day I had, not nineteen, but two hundred and forty-six signatures of honest sensible Englishmen to my petitions.

The only person under the stipulated age who signed it was Jack; he was not seventeen; but he wept, and implored so passionately for leave to tell the king not to let Romans make bad gods in England, that it would have been a sin to reject his protest. He rather cut than wrote his name on the parchment; the deepest crimson suffused his face, and his eyes flashed with the energy of his heartfelt protest against the abomination that he so well knew. He does not now regret it, while waiting for the summons to rejoice with the heavens, and the holy apostles and prophets, over the fall of Babylon the Great.

Our petition was presented to the Commons by the county member; to the Lords by the Bishop of London; and to the King by the noble, honest, protesting Duke of Newcastle. My zealous neighbour took them to London, and saw the first laid on the table, as he told me, with tears of thankfulness that he had been permitted to aid in the work. There are many, very many such men, of a class most respectable, but who lack the opportunity of engaging in causes that their inmost hearts approve; and there are many ladies who, if they knew how to find such active and trusty agents, would not sit idle as they do, and see their country perish for lack of a little enterprize like the foregoing. Two people in each parish throughout England as much in earnest as we were, might have frightened the treacherous betrayers of our national fortress from their unhallowed deed; OR MIGHT AT THIS VERY TIME ARREST THE PROGRESS OF OUR DECAY. We possess a machinery of almost boundless power: but we are too lazy to set the wheels in motion. I bless God for his infinite mercy in directing me to a line of action that has enabled me, in every fresh announcement of wrong inflicted on the Protestants of Ireland, and dangers accumulating round the very heart of England, to say, "I am free from the blood of all men." It was no more than a most imperative duty: its omission would have been no less than a very grievous sin; but that duty I was enabled to perform; that sin I was enabled to escape; and with the sense of it warm on my heart I say to you and to others, "Go, and do likewise."

But the national offence was not to be averted by a few instances of practical Protestantism, and as the time drew near my anguish of spirit was very great. I have staid up nearly all the night, making like Daniel, with tears my supplications unto the Lord, that he would pardon the sin of our princes and rulers, and have mercy on my people. Yet more; the two days that preceded it I caused to be kept as so strict a fast, that nothing but bread and potatoes entered the house. It was the only time that I ever in my life made it compulsory on others to fast; but they did it willingly, for nobody under that roof could be ignorant how awful was the stake impending.

And here I have to name one whom it is to me a privilege even to name. When a few distracted lines from my hand apprized a valued military friend in Jersey of the dreadful loss I had sustained in my dear brother, a guest, connected with his family, was present, who took the pen, and wrote me instantly a letter full of the richest, the tenderest, and sweetest consolation that ever overflowed from even the warm heart of Hugh M'Neile. I felt it powerfully; and when, not long after, he visited us, to pour yet farther the balm of Christian sympathy on the wound, I saw what a treasure the Lord was giving me in such a friend, and I cannot tax myself now with having ever undervalued the blessing. At the fearful crisis in question, on the eve of passing that wicked bill, Mr. M'Neile published his memorable pamphlet, entitled "England's Protest is England's shield." I did not see it until the very time arrived, and I remember sitting up the whole night after reading it, pondering on the picture that he had drawn, of consequences following upon a sin the very model of which was set forth, and its punishment also awfully declared, in the book of Jeremiah. Alas! how often have the feet of our rulers been found "stumbling on the dark mountains!"—while they looked for light, how often has it been turned into the shadow of death, since the warning was despised, and the Lord's favoured people took into close alliance the idolatrous abomination that incenses him! We were then called alarmists, bigots, prejudiced fanatics; and well do I remember the stress laid on an argument that influenced many an upright character. "Supposing," it was urged, "that an oath of fidelity to the interests of a Protestant government would not be considered binding by members of the Romish Church, do you imagine that a company of GENTLEMEN would violate their pledged word of honour!" This told well with men of the world; and not a few Christians were led away by it, so that the clamour excited against the impugners of Romish integrity was very trying to meet, and numbers shrank from their protest, because it implied a charge against the private character of individuals who had done nothing to merit such suspicion. There were those, however, and among men of most delicate mind, incapable of indicting a needless wound, who could not thus be deterred from uttering their convictions, since too fully verified, that no bond could hold a true Romanist neutral or inactive, when once a question arose, touching the opposite interests of the hostile system. Mr. M'Neile always proceeded on the simple fact that Popery is Antichrist; that in all things it must be the object of Antichrist to oppose and subvert the kingdom of Christ; and that every subject of Antichrist must necessarily desire his master's advancement and do his master's bidding. The event has shewn how correct were his deductions; and he, who to this moment stands foremost within the fortress in resisting at every step the foe whom he could not repel from its walls, has earned a preeminence in their hatred that bespeaks better than anything else can do, the value of his services in the cause of truth.

The bill passed in the Commons, and still we clang to a hope that the noble warrior who had once been the instrument of saving his country would not now deliberately sell her into the hands of foreign foes:—sell her for a fuller measure of popularity, or for a little treacherous repose. Still more did we hope that God would preserve the bishops of the church from conniving at the sacrilegiously suicidal blow. Nay, it was more than a connivance: for had they been unanimously true to their church, there were a very large majority of the peers who would never have ventured to vote against them in a matter so nearly touching the cause which the lords spiritual were in that house expressly to judge and to defend. I confess I built much upon the bench; and a poor foundation it proved to be! A solemn note of prophetic warning was sounded by the Archbishop of Tuam on behalf of Ireland; echoed by our own metropolitan and others in reference to England, but in vain. The sun of our national greatness had passed its meridian, and, in the memorable words of honest Lord Eldon, began to set. The sin of the British parliament was consummated.

Nothing remained but to give the royal assent; and still would hope whisper that the prayers, if not the example of his father might prevail to deter the king of England from casting its independent diadem once more before the papal footstool. Here again the defection of the bishops operated most fatally: George the Fourth would not have ratified the surrender, if their influence, public and private, had been duly exerted to withhold him from it. The pen was put into a reluctant hand; a hasty scratch with that pen undid the work of the Revolution; and so far as man could accomplish it, of the Reformation also.

I cannot describe to you the feeling with which I learned that all was thus lost. It did not partake of resignation; it did not include the smallest portion of acquiescence. God forbid! Some of my pious friends, who had felt with me all along, received the tidings with devout submission, saying, "The will of the Lord be done!" My amen to this aspiration had a clause added to it; I could only repeat, "The will of the Lord be done, by the undoing of what is so outrageously opposed to his known will!" I no more assented to the act than I would have assented to a murder: I no more regarded it as the Lord's doing than I regarded the setting up of the golden calves at Dan as his doing. Permitted by the Lord it was: for he often permits nations, like individuals, to destroy themselves by committing presumptuous sins; but is he therefore the author, the abettor, or the approver of their crimes? assuredly not. So far must we submit to the ordinances of man as not to raise a rebellious hand against their execution; but to look placidly on while the abomination of desolation is set up to stand where the Lord expressly says "IT OUGHT NOT," and to conclude that he wills it to stand there because he did not wither the hands employed in fixing it, is a stretch of indifferentism to which I hope I shall never be able to attain. No: the "atrocious bill," as it was rightly termed, became the law of England; but inasmuch as it is wholly opposed to the law of God, let us see to it that our protest against its continuance on our statute-book be fully as powerful, as persevering, as was our protest against its entrance there.

The usual lapse of some days between the signing of a new act and its coming into force, threw the first operation of the Popish bill upon a day remarkable as being that of a nominal saint of England. A most Popish coincidence! to enhance which the reigning monarch had adopted the Popish custom of celebrating the festival of St. George, in April, as his birthday, which really occurred in August; calling it his name-day, after the continental mode. To these strangely concurrent circumstances was added one yet more striking; namely, the fact that the noted Pastorini had predicted many years before, that the great effectual blow against Protestantism would be struck on the 14th of April, 1829:—the 13th of April, 1829, was the day on which the royal assent crowned the notorious bill!

I have alluded before to an abbé, an aged French priest who held a professorship at the Royal Military College; an amiable kind-hearted old man, who retired at this time from his situation, and went to end his years in his native land. It happened that the 23rd was fixed for his departure, and as I sat in deep dejection in my study, grieving over the changed aspect of my country, now that the antichristian law was come into full force, I saw the old man, full of national vivacity, walk briskly past, on his way to make inquiries respecting a coach. The sight of his silver locks, shining in the sunbeam, and the conviction that he was probably going beyond the reach of Christian privileges, melted me. I seized a pen, and wrote him a most earnest letter, faithfully setting before him the fearfulness of that delusion in which he was not only himself wrapped, but daily wrapping up the souls of others—

for he officiated as priest in the place. I implored him to read God's word: I assured him how cordially I concurred in the declaration of his Church, that either he or I was certainly on the road to hell; for that two paths directly opposed to each other could not possibly end in the same place: I told him that my own confidence of safety and salvation was grounded solely on the revealed, infallible word of God: and I charged him as he must face me at the judgment-seat of Christ, to search diligently into that sure and safe directory as to the bearing of his own path. I wrote affectionately, with many tears, and fervent prayers; and enclosing with the letter a present of books, had it given to him as he mounted the coach. Whether the Lord blessed, or may yet bless it to him, I know not: I hope I delivered my own soul. After this, which indeed proved a great relief to my oppressed feelings, I took my little nephew and sallied forth for a walk. It was a glorious day; the sun shone with surpassing brilliancy from a cloudless sky; and the fresh breeze had all the softness of advanced spring. I strolled through a grove of oaks, pondering on the naval greatness of my country, on the vaunted "Hearts of oak" that both formed her fleets and manned them, and bewailing the infatuation that had now planted a deadly Upas in the midst of her fair national garden. Every object around me seemed to speak reproach, from the peaceful beauty of that fearless repose in which for so many centuries our happy isle had lain beneath the shadow of the Lord's hand. "I have nourished and brought up children, and they have rebelled against me," was the purport of the voice that seemed to breathe rebuke. Wandering on, I came to the winding rampart of the college, a beautifully-retired walk, where mounds of earth, covered with rich grass, aid the military effect of that fine establishment; and here a turn brought me at once upon an object calculated to wound me beyond all the rest.

It was the royal standard of England, hoisted in honour of the king's name-day: an immense banner of rich silk, splendidly emblazoned with the well-known arms. England's three lions in the proud attitude of menacing advance; Scotland's rampant one rejoicing in his independence: and poor Ireland's neglected harp, once tuned to the highest strains of inspired psalmody; now for many a long age perverted to the service of idols, and polluted by the licentious fingers of those who work on the passions of her children to rivet more deeply the fetter on their souls—all these were unrolled before me, just then drooping in a lull of the breeze; and the Irish quarter partially resting on a mound of green sod, where it lay, languid and sad. I leaned against the opposite bank, weeping most abundantly as I gazed; for all the chivalrous feelings of former days were awakened to embitter the rest. How often had my heart beat joyously while I looked upon that noble standard, floating on the 4th of June, the birthday of good old George the Third, whose prayerful fidelity to his sacred trust kept that flag secure, uncontaminated, victorious, through his sixty years' reign! And that head which he was ready to lay on a block rather than surrender the sacred protest, was mouldering with the dead—his son *had* surrendered it—our protest was gone! I could not quite realize the fact, it appeared so incredible to me, after all I had read of the past and all I had seen in Ireland of the workings of Popery wherever it could snatch even momentary power. But the wind freshened again, the heavy folds of the gorgeous banner slowly rose upon it, all its bright blazonry stood out in wonted pride, unconscious of the "Ichabod" that sacrilegious hands had written on every trophy, and with a fresh burst of tears I turned away.

For all this, and for the deep despondency that oppressed me then, I was rebuked, of course, by man: but God never rebuked me for it. Twelve years have elapsed, and each year has heaped upon us a fresh load of that "fruit of our own ways," which will crush us at last. That "healing measure," as its expediency-mongering patrons loved to call it, did indeed heal the deadly wound of the Beast among us, and bade him again live, to our confusion. Ireland is all but given up as an uncontested prey to him; her Protestant church dismantled, her Protestant Bible mutilated, her Protestant corporations disbanded, her Protestant landlords massacred as a matter of course; and the very Union, any attempt at infringing which is high treason, made the object of unmasked attacks on the part of a man who has armed and marshalled her millions in open rebellion against the British government, which, judicially given over to infatuation, fawns on his person and courts his patronage. In England, disaffection to the crown combined with and strengthened by principles of gross infidelity, an increasing contempt of old institutions because they are based on Christianity, an open scorn of the Sabbath, and an immense falling away to popery in the mass of the people; while within the church, even in its pulpits and among its distinguished ministers, prevails a revival of more than semi-papal error, such as must wholly destroy the spiritual life of that body if it be not speedily and summarily checked. Instead of this, we too well know that it is daily extending, bearing in itself the seeds of a future and cruel persecution of God's people. We cannot look on these things and deny that they have come upon us in just retribution for 1829; we cannot, without expecting at the Lord's hand such a compromise of his Majesty and truth as he will never make, look for deliverance from these fears and dangers, until we have, by a national act, put away the evil of those doings which have provoked him to forsake us.

LETTER XIV.

EMPLOYMENT.

*   *   *

In the village where I lived, there was a very good National school, well attended; also a Sunday-school; and the poorer inhabitants generally were of a respectable class, with many of a higher grade, such as small tradesmen, and the families of those in subordinate offices about the Military College. I always took a great interest in the young; and as love generally produces love, there was no lack of affectionate feeling on their part. It occurred to me, as the Sunday was much devoted by most of them to idling about, that assembling such of them as wished it at my cottage would afford an opportunity for scriptural instruction; and without any thing resembling a school, or any regular proposal, I found a little party of six or seven children assembled in the afternoon, to hear a chapter read, answer a few questions upon it, and join in a short prayer. Making it as cheerful and unrestrained as possible, I found my little guests greatly pleased; and on the next Sabbath my party was doubled, solely through the favourable report spread by them. One had asked me, "Please, Ma'am, may I bring my little sister?" and on the reply being given, "You may bring any body and every body you like," a general beating up for recruits followed. In three or four weeks my assemblage amounted to sixty, only one half of whom could be crowded into the parlour of my small cottage. What was to be done? The work was rather arduous but as I too had been complaining not long before of having little to do for the Lord, except with the pen, I resolved to brave some extra labour. I desired the girls to come at four, the boys at six, and allowing an interval of half an hour between, we got through it very well. A long table was placed across the room, from corner to corner; round this they were seated, each with a Bible, I being at the head of the table. I found this easy and sociable way of proceeding highly gratified the children: they never called, never thought it a great school—they came bustling in with looks of great glee, particularly the boys, and greeted me with the affectionate freedom of young friends. A few words of introductory prayer were followed by the reading of one or more chapters, so that each had a verse or two; and then we talked over the portion of scripture very closely, mutually questioning each other. Many of the girls were as old as sixteen or seventeen, beautiful creatures, and very well dressed: and what a privilege it was to gather and so to arm them in a place where, alas! innumerable snares beset their path. We concluded with a hymn; and long before the half-hour had expired that preceded the boys' entrance, they were clustering like bees at the gate, impatient for the joyous rush; and to seat themselves round their dear table, with all that free confidence without which I never could succeed in really commanding the attention of boys.

Our choice of chapters was peculiar. I found they wanted stirring subjects, and I gave them Gideon, Samson, Jonathan, Nehemiah, Boaz, Mordecai, Daniel, and all the most manly characters of Old Testament history, with the rich gospel that lies wrapped in every page of that precious volume. Even in the new Testament I found that individualizing as much as possible the speaker or the narrative produced great effects. Our blessed Lord himself, John Baptist, Paul—all were brought before them as vividly as possible; and I can assure those who try to teach boys as they would teach girls that they are pursuing a wrong method. Mine have often coaxed an extra hour from me; and I never once saw them willing to go, during the fifteen months of our happy meetings. If the least symptom of unruliness appeared, I had only to tell them they were my guests, and I appealed to their feelings of manliness, whether a lady had not some claim to forbearance and respect. Nothing rights a boy of ten or twelve years like putting him on his manhood; and really my little lads became great gentlemen in mind and manners, while, blessed be God! not a few became, I trust, wise unto salvation. Their greatest temptation to disorderly doings was in the laughable, authoritative style of Jack's superintendence. He was now rapidly fading, but in mind brighter than ever. Seated in a large chair, a little to the rear of me, he kept strict watch over the party, and any deviation from what he considered correct conduct was noticed with a threat of punishment, conveyed by pinching his own ear, slapping his own face, kicking out his foot, and similar indications of chastisement, with a knowing nod at the offender. But if he saw an approach to levity over the word of God, his manner wholly changed. Tears filled his eyes, he looked all grief and entreaty, and the words, "God see," were earnestly spelled on his uplifted hands. No one could stand the appeal; and very rarely had he occasion to make it. I am sure his prayers helped forward the work mightily. It was wonderful to see thirty-two robust, boisterous fellows, from nine to seventeen years old, sitting in perfect delight and perfect order, for two and even three hours, on a fine Sunday evening, never looking dissatisfied till they were told to go.

I cannot help recording an event on which I look back with great thankfulness; though it was a terrible trial to me at the time. Two of my boys had a quarrel one week-day. One of them was very teasing, the other very passionate. The latter ran to a butcher's window close by, seized the large knife, and plunged it into the left side of his companion. Most mercifully, the wound was not dangerous; the keenness of the knife was in his favour; it penetrated to within a short distance of his heart, but separated no large vein, and within a few days the boy was out again. The Sunday after it occurred my party were exceedingly moved; they expressed great anger, and not a few threats were uttered against the culprit, whose parents had locked him up. On the following Sabbath I resolved to make an effort to avoid bad consequences, and also to arrest the poor boy in his dangerous course. He had rather justified himself than otherwise, and had shown a spirit sadly unsubdued, and unthankful for his escape from a deadly crime and its awful consequences. I sent word to him to come to my party: he replied he would not. I repeated the summons, saying I should be exceedingly hurt if he did not. No answer was returned. The place next but one to me belonged to the wounded boy, that below it to his assailant; and the former was present, pale indeed, but well. I lost no time in announcing to them that I expected P., which occasioned a burst of indignation, some saying they would not stay in the room with him, and the rest seeming to assent. "Then," said I, "you must go, for he wants instruction most; and the very feeling that makes you shrink from associating with him proves that you are better taught. So if you will leave me, do; I must admit him." Just then P. was seen coming down the little garden: he entered, his walk very erect, his eyes unflinching, and his dark brows knitted. The looks of my young lads were very eloquent; his bold bearing exasperated them much. My heart seemed bursting its boundary with the violent palpitation of alarm, and other emotions which I could scarcely suppress; but I motioned to P. to take his usual place, and instantly rising offered up the usual prayer, with a petition for the spirit of mutual compassion, forgiveness and love. I ceased, all remaining standing and certainly it was a period of most fearful interest. I looked imploringly at the wounded boy; he hesitated for a moment, then suddenly turned, and with an air of noble frankness held out his hand to P., who took it directly. I then offered him mine; he grasped it, and burst into tears. A delightful scene followed, each pressing to seal his forgiveness in the same manner, while Jack's countenance shone with almost heavenly beauty on a spectacle so congenial to his loving heart. We had a most happy evening, and I could not but tell my dear boys how much I rejoiced over them. Whatever may have been the effect on the characters of those concerned, I know not.* I am persuaded the proceeding was a means of averting much mischief. Boys are noble creatures when placed on their right footing; but I always think there is a great deal too much of what is technically termed old womanism in the mode of conducting their scriptural education. They are pugnacious animals too, and require prudent management. News was brought me one evening, while they waited for admission, that two of them had stripped off their jackets to fight, the dispute being which loved their teacher most. "Exclude them both to-night," said a friend, "and threaten to expel them." Instead of which I sent word that the one who first put on his jacket loved me most, and that I was ready to begin. In they both came, smiling, and they got their lecture in due time, when a passage in point came before us.

Now, who complains of non-employment while England has so many neglected lambs of her fold to gather, and so many who, in the dull routine of a school, get only a mechanical knowledge of what would deeply interest them if brought before them with the help of a little personal condescension and care. It is a branch of Christian duty for which all are competent who know the Gospel; and two, three, or four young people invited to come in for an hour or so at stated times, to sit down at a table and *talk* over the passages of scripture which may appear best calculated to engage their pleased attention, may often prove the foundation for a noble work. It is particularly needed now, when information is universally sought after; and be it remembered, I am also speaking of a class above the very poor. They are a most important class, as we shall soon find; for from them are the Chartist bodies officered, and active agents supplied in works of infinite mischief. False pride will interpose, no doubt. We like better to deal with those a good way removed, than with such as may claim a comparative approximation to our new rank;

* Since the first edition was printed, I have heard of P.'s death and that he died in the faith.

and the devil desires no better auxiliary to his designs than the pride of which he is the loving father. Again, ladies do not like to instruct boys: they are very wrong. Female influence is a powerful thing, and frequently exerted for evil—why not for good? We brought all the sin into the world, involving man in the ruin that he was not the first to seek; and it is the least we can do to offer him a little good now. I never yet met a boy— and thanks be to God I have taught many—who would be rude to a female, earnestly and kindly seeking his welfare without attempting to crush that independence of spirit which is man's prerogative, and which no woman has a right to crush.

I need not say that in the foregoing, and in all similar works wherein the Lord permitted me to engage, I laboured diligently to make my young friends something more than nominal Protestants. To omit this, in giving instruction, is the very madness of inconsistent folly and cruelty.

A few weeks after the commencement of my weekly assemblages I was called to the metropolis in search of medical aid for a dear child of my brother's. I found it, and all that Christian kindness could add to render it doubly valuable, at the hands of an estimable physician, near whom I resolved to stay for a few weeks; and while secretly lamenting that here at least I should find nothing to do, an answer was given to my unbelief that might well shame it. To the same end, I will record this also, the circumstances being already well known, but not the delightful encouragements that are afforded when a project is entered upon in single, simple reliance on the help of Him for whose glory his people desire to work. Unbelief in his *willingness*—for we dare not doubt his *power*, to prosper our poor attempts—is the real bar to all success. Such mistrust is infinitely dishonouring to him.

Six years had elapsed since I left Ireland, but my affection for the country and people was unchanged, and unchangeable. The very centre of the isle had become the grave of my beloved brother, and this only added tenfold to the touching interest excited by the very mention of that land. Strange to say, I had never heard of the Irish Society, nor considered of what vast importance it would be to make the language of the natives a medium of conveying spiritual instruction to them. The annual meeting was about to be held, and among the Irish clergymen forming the deputation to London was the Rev. Charles Seymour, the venerable and every way estimable pastor under whose ministry my brother had been placed at Castlebar, and from whom I had received letters fully confirmatory of my sanguine hope that he had indeed and wholly embraced the Gospel of Christ. Longing to see Mr. Seymour, I went to him on the morning of the meeting; and most sweet was the testimony he had to give; most tender the sympathy he evinced in all my sorrow and all my gladness. After a conversation that left me overflowing with gratitude for the blessings vouchsafed to my precious brother, he asked me to attend the meeting, and I went prepared to take a lively interest in whatever might be said respecting Ireland. How great was my astonishment when for the first time I heard the story of Bishop Bedell, of the Irish Bible, and of the good work in rapid progress among the Aborigines of the land. The extent and inveteracy of the disease I well knew; but the suitability of the remedy had never been set before me. In fact, I hardly knew that the Irish was a written language; and strange it seemed to have passed three years in a part of the country where it is extensively spoken, and in the house of one who always conversed in that tongue with the rustic frequenters of her shop, yet to be so grossly ignorant of all relating to it. I resolved to become an active partizan of the Irish Society in Ireland; but a different turn was soon given to my sympathies. Mr. Seymour spoke after the others; he said much, calculated to prove the power of the language in preaching the Gospel; but suddenly reverting to the state of the many thousands of his poor countrymen congregated in London, he drew a most affecting picture of their destitute, degraded condition. He appealed to us as Christians; and reminding us of our many privileges, bade us take care that the souls of his poor countrymen did not rise up in judgment to condemn us for allowing them to perish in the heart of our metropolis. "Open," he said, "a bread-shop in St. Giles's; deal forth a little of the bread of life to their starving souls. Ye English Christians, I appeal to you for them: oh, pity my poor lost countrymen, open but a bread-shop in St. Giles's!" Tears ran down his venerable face, as he lifted his clasped hands, and bent towards us. The effect of his words on me was electric: I looked at him, and silently but fervently said, "So God help me as I will open you a bread-shop in St. Giles's if He does but permit!" again and again did I repeat the pledge; and when Lord Roden spoke— the first time of my seeing that noble Irishman—and heartily seconded the appeal, I renewed the secret promise, with such purpose of heart as rarely fails to accomplish its object.

For some days I tried in vain to do anything towards it; but on the Sunday, passing from Great Russell-street to Long acre, through the worst part of St. Giles's, I saw the awful state of that district, and declared to my companion, himself a devoted Irishman, my fixed resolve to have a church there. He warmly encouraged it, extravagant as the idea appeared; and I began to pray earnestly for direction from above. Two nights after, a thought struck me; I wrote an appeal on behalf of the miserable Irish Papists in that place, likening their case among us to that of Lazarus lying at the rich man's gate and imploring means to give them the gospel in their own tongue. This I had printed, and sent copies as I could to various friends. Some smiled at my enthusiasm; others pointed out the work among distant heathens as far more important. Many wished me success; a few rebuked me for desiring to proselytize the members of another church; and still fewer gave me money. At the end of a fortnight's hard begging I had got just seven pounds towards building a Church! This was slow work. One day, dining at the table of my dear friend Dr. Pidduck, he heard many bantering me for being so sanguine, and said, "You remind me of Columbus, going to the cathedral of Seville to ask a blessing on his romantic project of discovering a new world. Every body laughed at him. Nevertheless, Columbus succeeded, *and so will you*." At that moment a gentleman sitting next me laid a sovereign on my piece of bread; and the coincidence of the gold and the "bread-shop," combined with the doctor's confident prediction, put new life into me;—I boldly said, "I WILL succeed."

With the sum of seven pounds in hand, I wrote to the Bishop of Lichfield and Coventry, begging him to ask the Bishop of London if he would licence my Irish church and an Irish clergyman if I provided both! Lord Mountsandford took this letter to him; and the next day he brought me this rather startling message:—"The Bishop of London will licence your church: Lichfield sends his love to you, and desires you will summon the gentlemen who are assisting you in this under-taking—half a dozen or so—to meet him in Sackville-street on Saturday next, and be there yourself. He will see what can be done to forward it." Half-a-dozen gentlemen! where was I to find them? My only helpers were Mr. Maxwell, Dr. Pidduck, and Lord Mountsandford himself. However, I went to work, praying incessantly, and solacing myself with that beautiful text, "Go up to the mountain and bring wood and build the house, and I will take pleasure in it, and I will be glorified, saith the Lord." I suppose I repeated that verse a hundred times a day in my solitude, attending the sick child, and writing letters till I nearly fell from my seat with exhaustion.

Saturday arrived: I had no idea how far my applications might have succeeded; but if I had as many gentlemen there as pounds in my treasury, namely seven, it would be sufficient. I went trembling with hope and fear, accompanied by two warm-hearted young Irish barristers, whom my good friend Mr. Maxwell had pressed into the service. Oh what could I render unto the Lord for all His goodness to me, when I saw the glorious spectacle presented to my view at the hour appointed! There sat the good Bishop Ryder in the chair; beside him the Bishop of Bath and Wells; Lords Lorton, Lifford, Bexley, Mountsandford, and Carberry; and of other clergymen and gentlemen upwards of forty. "Let us ask a blessing," said the Bishop of Lichfield: and when we all kneeled down to commit unto the LORD a work so new, so strange, and to poor human reason so hopelessly wild as this had appeared two days before, I thought I might as well die then as not: I could never die happier.

All was zeal, love, unanimity: they placed it on a good basis, and my seven pounds were multiplied by more than seven before we broke up. They did not take the work out of my hands, but formed themselves into a body for aiding in carrying it on: the rector of St. Giles' came forward voluntarily to give his hearty consent, and ten pounds; and if there was a pillow of roses in London that night, I surely slept on it. In six weeks my memorable seven pounds swelled to thirteen hundred; a church was bought, a pastor engaged, and a noble meeting held in Freemasons' Hall, to incorporate the new project with the Irish Society. I went back to Sandhurst elated with joy, and lost no time in putting up, most conspicuously written out on a card, over my study fire-place, the lines that I had so often repeated during the preceding two months

> "Victorious Faith the promise sees
>   And looks to God alone;
> Laughs at impossibilities
>   And says, "IT SHALL BE DONE."

In the following November the Irish Episcopal church in St. Giles' was opened for divine service on Advent Sunday, the Rev. H. H. Beamish officiating. A more eloquent and fluent preacher, a more gifted and devoted man, the whole church of God could not have supplied. He preached the whole gospel in Irish to the listening, wondering people, who hung with delight upon accents so dear to them; and he attacked their pestilent heresies with the bold faithfulness of one who meant what he said, when vowing to drive away all erroneous and strange doctrines from those under his charge. God blessed most richly his ministry: many were awakened, several truly converted to Christ, and not a small number fully convinced of the falsehood of their own superstition, which they forsook. We had forty communicants from among the most wretchedly ignorant and bigotted of the Irish Romanists, before

Mr. Beamish left his post: and one of them had even endured a cruel martyrdom for the truth's sake. A bread-shop indeed it was; and the old Christian, whose fervent appeal had given rise to its establishment, himself preached there in Irish to a delighted congregation before the Lord took him to Himself.

I must, however, go back to the period of my sojourn in London, to mention some other matters. Two especial blessings I obtained there: the ministry of Mr. Howels, and the friendship of one whom you well know by character as portrayed under the type of the Hearts'-Ease in the Chapters on Flowers, Mr. Donald. The two blessings were indeed one; for never were hearts more closely knit in brotherly love than those of Howels and Donald, now together before the throne of the Lamb. I cannot set forth what I owe to my pastor at Long Acre in the way of strengthening my faith against the perilous delusions of Irvingism, which were continually seeking to enwrap me; but which, by God's grace, I had been enabled to resist, at the commencement, by an appeal to my Bible alone: I must enter more fully upon that presently. The most valuable lesson, however, which I learned from Mr. Howels was, speaking out. Up to that time I had been very cautious, and refrained from touching on controversy; persuaded that to oppose error openly and directly, was an unsafe proceeding: I had attacked it covertly, rather by setting forth the light than by noticing the darkness, at least in my writings, and in speaking to the Romanists; but now I began to feel that to "contend earnestly for the faith once delivered to the saints," must necessarily include an open denunciation of the errors which subverted that faith. Mr. Howels was peculiarly bold and direct in his manner of preaching down heresy, in whatsoever form it lifted up its head; nor did he at all flinch from warning individuals. Contrary to the usual plan of gently insinuating what he intended to convey, he left no possibility of mistaking his meaning. I was greatly astonished, when, on the very first day of my attendance at Long Acre, he abruptly said from the pulpit, "I am accused of dealing too severely with individuals; they say I struck Irving too hard. *I* strike Irving! No, he struck himself, I did not strike him; who would strike a suicide?" He proceeded to exhibit the suicidal effects of those doctrines which Mr. Irving was then beginning to proclaim: and so completely was my attention rivetted by the undisguised personality with which he had commenced, that it was to me as the regular discussion of a particular case, instead of being lost in the generalizing effect of what might apply to almost anything. In like manner he dealt with Popery and with Socinianism, calling them by these their proper names, and specifying distinctly any man, living or dead, whose particular errors he was assailing. I found this manner of instructing most effectual: all that he said became, as it were, so classed in the memory, that each sentence was made available in the precise department to which it belonged. Through the goodness of God in teaching me out of his own blessed word, I had learned those truths which my pastor set forth; and there was no mistaken view, as I remember, on my part to be rectified by his instructions. I went along with him fully and cordially, in all things save one—the Second Advent—but incalculably did he strengthen me on points where before I indeed stood, but where now I felt that I stood fast; and I soon learned that to possess the weapons of a warfare into which the church was entering was not enough: they must be openly used. His very plain speaking, which shocked some fastidious tastes, showed me how much we lose by diluting our native Saxon; and I resolved by God's grace to make a better use in future of my mother-tongue.

In warning my young Sabbath-party against Popery, I had been used to say, "There are some mistaken people who will pay honour to those which are no gods: doing superstitious things, and so forth," describing the observances of the Romish system. Now, I at once addressed them without circumlocution: "Papists, who are by some foolishly and falsely called Catholics, are taught by their priests the most idolatrous, antichristian things possible;" and then proceeded to shew those things. This had the effect I expected; it embodied an idea otherwise vague and indistinct; and ensured their remembering the particular errors when they should meet with the party named. To the Romanist himself I learned to be equally explicit, not merely combatting idolatry as before, by dwelling on the command to worship God alone, but at once branding as idolatrous specific acts habitually committed by those of his communion; and showing at one view the actual sin with the divine prohibition of it. This is controversy; and so long as the world lieth in wickedness the church *must* be a controversial body: this is proselytizing; and so long as men are to be turned from darkness to light, we *must* proselytize. At the outset of my efforts for an Irish church in St. Giles's it was objected by one or two friends, "You want to make proselytes." I answered, "No; we only want to preach the gospel." A very few Sundays at Long Acre however changed my tone, and thenceforth the reply was, "To be sure we do; of what avail will the preaching of Christ be, if it does not overthrow the dominion of Antichrist?" At a subsequent period, an Irish reader of mine asked me, "Ma'am, do you forbid me to speak controversially?" "Certainly not: shew the people their errors, as set forth by the Holy Spirit for that very purpose of convincing them of the sin." "I am thankful to hear you say that, Ma'am. Some of the gentlemen charge me never to engage in controversy, but how can I help it? When I was a Papist, I read the Bible because it was the only book in Irish that I could well teach my pupils out of; and I did it without being at all unsettled in my false religion, until I was teaching Miss——— and she stopped me whenever we came to a strong passage against idolatry and the like, saying, 'Now, Mr.——— how do you reconcile that with your religion?' I was very mad at her, and strove to forget it; but I could not get the words out of the Bible, and they troubled my conscience, till at last I took to comparing Popery with what she had told me was written to warn me out of it: and by God's blessing out I came." Another said, "I might have read fifty times over, 'The blood of Jesus Christ cleanseth from all sin,' and not objected to it, and still remained a Papist: but a Protestant pointed it out, and said, 'If the *blood of Christ* cleanseth from all sin, what are your works, your penances, your expiatory masses good for? And if the blood of Jesus Christ cleanseth from *all* sin, what more has purgatory to do for the soul? And if there be no purgatory, what becomes of the infallibility of your church? And if your church be not infallible, what leg have you got to stand upon?' I felt, continued the narrator, as if the ground was cleaving under my feet; and from that time I never rested till I had come to Christ for the blood of sprinkling, and cast my idols to the moles and the bats." So much for controversy.

I have noticed that I did not go with Mr. Howels on the subject of the Second Advent: I could not. In fact, I was a millennarian against my will. The three particulars on which I did not believe myself to be convinced, were, the vengeful dispensation against the Lord's enemies preparatory to the thousand years of blessedness; the literal nature of the first, premillennial resurrection; and the personal reign. With regard to the first, I wished to believe that the gospel would be universally victorious, subduing every heart, and bringing the whole world in peaceful submission to acknowledge the Lord as King. I had once, as before stated, been startled by a reference to the sixty-third of Isaiah, and lolled to sleep again by the far-fetched comments of good Matthew Henry: and I confess I had taken up the missionary cause on the gratuitous assumption that we were to convert every body, and could not agree to a less extensive triumph. Well, I did not choose to bring this to the test of scripture, because I did not wish to be undeceived; but just after the Irish meeting, one was held in reference to the Jews, at which I was present; and forth stepped my valued friend M'Neile, whom I had not seen for a year, and with his little bible in his hand preached the obnoxious doctrine, to my infinite annoyance and conviction. He took up my precise objection without knowing it: he spoke of those who could not see that a part of God's *mercy* was his *judgment*; and with that glowing ardour, tempered with deep solemnity, that always gives him so much of the prophetic

characteristic, if I may so speak, he read from the cxxxvi.
Psalm, "To Him that smote Egypt in their first-born; *for his*
MERCY *endureth for ever.*" "To Him which smote great kings: for
his MERCY *endureth for ever.* And slew mighty kings, *for his*
MERCY *endureth for ever.*" This was the key-note of a strain that
I deeply felt resounded through the whole scripture, though I
had refused to heed it; and then he turned to the lxi. of
Isaiah, and read the first and part of the second verse, as
quoted by our blessed Lord in the iv. of St. John, to where he
shut the book, saying, "this day is *this* scripture fulfilled in
your ears." But did the scripture end here? No: the first advent
fulfilled so much of it; and He who then proclaimed "the
acceptable year of the Lord," should at his second coming
proceed with that unfinished scripture,—"the day of vengeance of our God." And go on thence "To comfort all that
mourn: to appoint unto them that mourn in Zion,"—and so
the whole beautiful picture of millennial gladness and glory on
which Isaiah expatiates rose before me, as consequent upon
that "day of vengeance," which Christ has not yet in person
proclaimed. How angry I felt with that dauntless champion of
God's whole truth, for trampling upon my darling prejudices!
nevertheless he had done it; and thenceforth I opened my mind
to drink in the pure simple meaning of the literal promise.

The first resurrection I considered to be a resurrection of
the souls of the martyrs, whose spirits were to animate the
happy race of believers during a thousand years. I confess some
things puzzled me sorely in this interpretation: for instance,
how could a soul be buried; and if not buried how did it rise?
Again, those souls were under an altar in heaven, waiting for
the completion of their company by means of a new persecution on earth, and it seemed rather a heathenish doctrine to
transmigrate them into other bodies, more especially as their
own bodies would need them again. Besides, they were with
Christ personally in heaven; and to be without Christ, personally on earth, was by no means an additional privilege. I found
the thing untenable, and resolved to consider it as wholly figurative; but if so, then the final judgment, described also in that

chapter, might be figurative too. I could not look my own inferences in the face; so I wished to let the subject alone; but then a blessing was distinctly pronounced on such as should read or hear the words of that prophecy; and I did not like to lose a blessing.

Thus the matter stood. I had rigidly forborne to read any book, pro or con, or to be talked to about it. One day, when the subject forced itself on me, I resolved to strengthen myself against the modern view (as I widely supposed it) by prayerfully reading again what I already so well knew—the xv. chapter of I Corinthians. I did so: and was suddenly struck by a recollection of the passage where the "saying" is written, "Death is swallowed up in victory." I turned to Isaiah xxv., read it, and found it unequivocally a description of the Church's blessedness on earth—the millennium—at the outset of which the saying is written which "shall come to pass" when Christ's people rise from the dead. But will not all rise then? I went over the apostle's description once more, and found no word of the resurrection unto condemnation. The corruptible then raised would all put on incorruption; the weakness, power; the mortal, immortality: having borne the image of the earthly, they were to bear the image of the heavenly. I was quite overpowered: could I reply against God? The passage that I thought so formidable on my side failed me—"Afterwards they that are Christ's at his coming. *Then* cometh the end." But an interval of a thousand years might surely precede that "Then," since more than eighteen hundred have intervened since "the acceptable year of the Lord," and we have not yet seen "the day of vengeance of our God," though only a comma separates them in the Bible. From this starting point I explored the Scriptures in reference to a literal resurrection of Christ's people, at a literal coming previous to the thousand years of Satan's binding and the peace of the church. I saw it clearly: I received it fully: and I hold it firmly at this day.

On the continued personal presence of the Lord Jesus during that period I was much longer undecided; but I received it gradually, as necessary to the harmonious completion of the whole. I shall have occasion to mention it again. Whenever Mr. Howels took up this subject of the Second Advent, I was more than willing to be convinced, or rather unconvinced by him; but I could not. He always lost his temper, talked of sending the millennarians to a lunatic asylum; but never showed cause for their commitment to such safe custody. Donald was by no means favourable to the view, and once asked me "Why do you hold this mistaken opinion?" I answered playfully, "Because it is the only subject on which Howels talks nonsense." He shook his head, and said, "I candidly tell you, I wish he would let it alone." He did not, however, let it be alone; and had he been spared to us to this day, he would, I doubt not, have been found among its most powerful proclaimers.

It has often struck me what efforts the enemy has made to stifle this doctrine. The check given by Irvingism was very great, and though it did not lead me to question what I found in my Bible, it made me very cautious in receiving, very backward in declaring, any further light on the subject. Two years later, a valuable Christian clergyman who had received, and alas! still holds those deluding errors, when lamenting my awful pertinacity in resisting them, and warning me of my supposed sin, added, "Nevertheless I have hope of you, my sister. You believe in the second advent: you will not be saved by your faith in a glorified Saviour." To which I answered, "I will not. I will be saved by my faith in a crucified Saviour. I believe in his glorious, pre-millennial coming, but it is his cross, not his crown, that saves my soul." This was considered the climax of heresy, and I was given over as lost.

But shall the abuse of the sublime truth by the great enemy lead us to reject it? As well may we blot out the ninety-first Psalm, because the devil quoted it, and for a truly devilish purpose. No: he knows that the shedding forth of greater light on this important branch of Christian knowledge is one of the signs of Christ's actual coming; a token that his own time is short; therefore he endeavours to stifle it; and ere long he will bring us false Christs, to deceive if it were possible, the very elect. We have need to be found watching!

LETTER XV.

DARKNESS AND LIGHT.

*　　*　　*

I return to the period of my delivering up a sacred trust into the hands of Him who had committed it to me. Jack had lingered long, and sunk very gradually; but now he faded apace. His eldest sister, a very decided Romanist, came over for the purpose of seeing him, and to take care that he had "the rites of the church." Had the Abbé remained, it is probable we should have soon found ourselves deep in controversy: for, as priest, he never should have crossed my threshold, to bring upon my house the curse attached to idolatrous worship; but he was gone, and there was happily no other within reach. Jack requested me to promise him in his sister's presence that no Romish priest should come near him: I willingly did so; and moreover informed her that if she was herself dying and asked for one, he would not be admitted under my roof. The "abomination that maketh desolate" stands in many places where it ought not, but where I have authority it never did; nor by God's grace ever shall. I have toleration full and free for every form of Christianity, but none for Antichrist, come in what form he may.

It may be possible to describe a glorious summer sunset, with all the softening splendour that it sheds around; but to describe the setting of my dumb boy's sun of mortal life is impossible. He declined like the orb of day, gently, silently, gradually, yet swiftly, and gathered new beauties as he approached the horizon. His sufferings were great, but far greater his patience; and nothing resembling a complaint ever escaped him. When appearing in the morning, with pallid, exhausted looks, if asked whether he had slept, he would reply, with a sweet smile, "No, Jack no sleep; Jack think good Jesus Christ see poor Jack. Night dark; heaven all light: soon see heaven. Cough much now, pain bad: soon no cough, no pain." This was his usual way of admitting how much he suffered, always placing in contrast the glory to be revealed in him, and which seemed already revealed to him. Knowing that his recovery ʼwas impossible, I refrained, with his full concurrence, from having him tormented with miscalled alleviations, such as opiates, blood-letting, and so forth. All that kindness and skill could effect was gratuitously done for him, and everything freely supplied, by our medical friends; but they admitted that no permanent relief could be given, and I always hold it cruel to embitter the dying season with applications that in the end increase the sufferings they temporarily subdue. This plan kept the boy's mind clear and calm: the ever-present Saviour being to him instead of all soothing drugs. Sometimes when greatly oppressed, he has had leeches; and I remember once half-a-dozen were put on his side, at his own request. The inflammation was very great; the torture dreadful as they drew it to the surface and I was called to him, as he sat, grasping the arm of a chair, and writhing convulsively. He said to me, "Very, very pain: pain bad, soon kill;" and he seemed half wild with agony. Looking up in my face, he saw me in tears; and instantly, assumed his sweetest expression of countenance, saying in a calm, leisurely way, that his pain was much, but the pain the Lord suffered much more: his was only in his side; the Lord suffered in his side, his hands, his feet, and his head. His pain would be over in half an hour; the Lord's lasted many hours; he was "bad Jack," the Lord was "good Jesus Christ." Then again, he observed, the leeches made very little holes in his skin, and drew out a little blood; but the thorns, the nails, the spear, tore the Lord's flesh, and all his blood gushed out—it was shed to save him:

and he raised his eyes, lifted his clasped hands, turned his whole face up towards heaven, saying "Jack loves, loves, very loves good Jesus Christ!" When another violent pang made him start and writhe a little, he recovered in a moment, nodded his head, and said, "Good pain! make Jack soon go heaven."

His sublime idea of the "red hand" was ever present. He had told me some years before, that when he had lain a good while in the grave, God would call aloud, "Jack!" and he would start, and say, "Yes, me Jack." Then he would rise, and see multitudes standing together, and God sitting on a cloud with a very large book in his hand—he called it "Bible book"— and would beckon him to stand before him while he opened the book, and looked at the top of the pages, till he came to the name of John Britt. In that page, he told me, God had written all his "bads," every sin he had ever done; and the page was full. So God would look, and strive to read it, and hold it to the sun for light, but it was all "No, no, nothing, none." I asked him in some alarm if he had done no bad? He said yes, much bads; but when he first prayed to Jesus Christ he had taken the book out of God's hand, found that page, and pulling from his palm something which he described as filling up the hole made by the nail, had allowed the wound to bleed a little, passing his hand down the page so that, as he beautifully said, God could see none of Jack's bads, only Jesus Christ's blood. Nothing being thus found against him, God would shut the book, and there he would remain, standing before him, till the Lord Jesus came, and saying to God, "MY Jack," would put his arm round him, draw him aside, and bid him stand with the angels till the rest were judged.

All this he told me with the placid but animated look of one who is relating a delightful fact. I stood amazed, for rarely had the plan of a sinner's ransom, appropriation, and justifi-cation been so perspicuously set forth in a pulpit as here it was by a poor deaf and dumb peasant-boy, whose broken language was eked out by signs. He often told it to others; always making himself understood, and often have I seen the tears starting from a rough man's eye, as he followed the glowing representation. Jack used to sit silent and thoughtful for a long time together in his easy chair when too weak to move about; and then catching my eye, to say with a look of infinite satisfaction, "Good red hand!" I am persuaded that it was his sole and solid support: he never doubted, never feared, because his view of Christ's all-sufficiency was so exceedingly clear and realizing. It certainly never entered his head to question God's love to him. One night a servant went to his room, long after he had gone to bed: he was on his knees at the window, his hands and face held up towards a beautiful starlight sky. He did not perceive the servant's entrance: and next morning when I asked him about it, he told me that God was walking above, upon the stars; and that he went to the window and held up his head that God might look down into it and see how very much he loved Jesus Christ.

All his ideas were similar: all turned on the one theme so dear to them; and their originality was inexhaustible. What could be finer than his notion of the lightning, that it was produced by a sudden opening and shutting of God's eye— or of the rainbow, that it was the reflection of God's smile? What more graphic than his representation of Satan's malice and impotence, when, one evening, holding his finger to a candle, he snatched it back, as if burnt, pretending to be in great pain, and said, "Devil like candle." Then, with a sudden look of triumph, he added, "God like wind," and with a most vehement puff at once extinguished the light. When it was rekindled he laughed and said, "God kill devil."

He told me that God was always sitting still with the great book in his hand, and the Lord Jesus looking down for men, and crying to them, "Come man; come, pray." That the devil drew them back from listening, and persuaded them to spit up towards him, which was his sign for rebellion and contempt; but if at last a man snatched his hand from Satan, and prayed to the Lord Jesus, he went directly, took the book, found the name, and passed the "red hand" over the page, on seeing which Satan would stamp and cry. He gave very grotesque descriptions of the evil spirit's mortification, and always ended by bestowing on him a hearty kick. From seeing the effect, in point of watchfulness, prayer, and zeal, produced on this young Christian by such continual realization of the presence of the great tempter, I have been led to question very much the policy, not to say the lawfulness, of excluding that terrible foe as we do from our general discourse. It seems to be regarded as a manifest impropriety to name him, except with the most studied circumlocution, as though we were afraid of treating him irreverently; and he who is seldom named, will not often be thought of. Assuredly it is a great help to him in his countless devices to be so kept out of sight. We are prone to speak, to think, to act, as though we had only our own evil natures to contend with, including perhaps a sort of general admission that something is at work to aid the cause of rebellion; but it was far otherwise with Jack. If only conscious of the inward rising of a sullen or angry temper, he would immediately conclude that the devil was trying to make him grieve the Lord; and he knelt down to pray that God would drive him away. The sight of a drunken man affected him deeply: he would remark that the devil had drawn that man to the ale-house, put the cup into his hand with an assurance that God did not see, or did not care; and was now pushing him about to show the angels he had made that wretched being spit at the authority of the Lord. In like manner with all other vices, and some seeming virtues. As an instance of the latter, he knew a person who was very hostile to the Gospel, and to the best of his power hindered it, but who nevertheless paid the most punctual regard to all the formalities of external public worship. He almost frightened me by the picture he drew of that person's case, saying the devil walked to church with him, led him into a pew, set a hassock prominently forward for him to kneel on, put a handsome prayer-book into his hand; and while he carefully followed all the service, kept clapping him on the shoulder, saying, "A very good pray." I told this to a pious minister, who declared it was the most awfully just description of self-deluding formality, helped on by Satan, that ever he heard of. When partaking of the Lord's Supper, Jack told me that his feeling was,—"very, very love Jesus Christ; very, very *very* hate devil: go, devil!" and with holy indignation he motioned, as it were, the enemy from him. He felt that he had overcome the accuser by the blood of the Lamb. Oh that we all may take a lesson of wisdom from this simple child of God.

During the winter months he sank daily: his greatest earthly delight was in occasionally seeing Mr. Donald, for whom he felt the fondest love, and who seemed to have a presentiment of the holy union in which they would together soon rejoice before the Lord. Jack was courteous in manner, even to elegance: most graceful; and being now nineteen, tall and large, with the expression of infantine innocence and sweetness on a very fine countenance, no one could look on him without admiration; nor treat him with roughness or disrespect: but Donald's tenderness of manner was no less conspicuous than his; and I have watched that noble-minded Christian man waiting on the dying youth, as he sat patiently reclining in his chair—for he could not lie down—and the grateful humility with which every little kindness was received, until I almost forgot what the rude unfeeling world was like, in that exquisite contemplation. How much the fruit in God's garden is beautified by the process that ripens it!

Jack laboured anxiously to convert his sister and as he could not read at all, the whole controversy was carried on by signs. Mary was excessively mirthful. Jack unboundedly earnest; and when her playful reproaches roused his Irish blood, the scene was often very comic. I remember he was once bringing a long list of accusations against her priest, for taking his mother's money, making the poor fast, while the rich paid for dispensations to eat, inflicting cruel penances, drinking too much whiskey; and finally telling the people to worship wooden and breaden gods. To all this Mary attended with perfect good-humour, and then told him the same priest had christened him and made crosses upon him. Jack wrathfully intimated that he was then a baby, with a head like a doll's, and knew nothing; but if he had been wise he would have kicked his little foot into the priest's mouth. The controversy grew so warm that I had to part them. His horror of the priests was solely directed against their false religion; when I told him of one being converted, he leaped about for joy.

At the commencement of the year 1831 he was evidently dying; and we got a furlough for his brother to visit him. Poor Pat went to bed no more than twice during the fortnight he was there, so bitterly did he grieve over the companion of his early days; and many a sweet discourse passed between them on the subject of the blessed hope that sustained the dying Christian. He only survived Pat's departure four days. On the third of February the last symptoms came on; the death-damps began to ooze out, his legs were swelled to the size of his body, and he sat in that state, incapable of receiving warmth, scarcely able to swallow, yet clear, bright, and tranquil, for thirty hours. The morning of the last day was marked by such a revival of strength that he walked across the room with little help, and talked incessantly to me, and to all who came near him, He told me, among other things, that once God destroyed all men by rain, except those in the ark; and that he would soon do it again, not with water but with fire. He described the Lord as taking up the wicked by handfuls, breaking them, and throwing them into the fire; repeating, "all bads, all bads go fire." I ask if he was not bad; "Yes, Jack bad very." Would he be thrown into the fire? "No: Jesus Christ loves poor Jack." He then spoke rapturously of the "red hand," of the angels he should soon be singing with, of the day when Satan should be cast into the pit, and of the delight he should have in seeing me again. He prayed for his family, begged me to teach Mary to read the Bible, to warn Pat against bad examples, to bring up my brother's boys to love Jesus Christ, and lastly he repeated over and over again, the fervent injunction to love Ireland, to pray for Ireland, to write books for "Jack's poor Ireland," and in every way to oppose Popery. He called it "Roman" always; and it was a striking sight, to behold that youth all but dead, kindling into the most animated, stern, energetic warmth of manner, raising his cold, damp hands, and spelling with them the words "Roman is a lie." "One Jesus Christ, one (meaning he was the only Saviour) Jack's one Jesus Christ;" and then, with a force as if he would leave the characters impressed on his hands he reiterated, as slowly as possible, his dying Protest, "Roman is a LIE!" Very sweetly he had thanked me for all my care; and now he seemed to bequeath to me his zeal against the destroyer of his people. The last signs of removal came on in the evening; his sight failed, he rubbed his eyes, shook his head, and then smiled with conscious pleasure. At last he asked me to let him lie down on the sofa where he had been sitting, and saying very calmly, "A sleep," put his hand into mine, closed his eyes, and breathed his spirit forth so gently that it was difficult to mark the precise moment of that joyful change.

I still hope to throw into a volume the numerous particulars that remain untold concerning this boy and I will not now dwell upon the subject longer. God had graciously kept me faithful to my trust; and I surrendered it, not without most keenly feeling the loss of such a companion, but with a glow of adoring thankfulness that overcame all selfish regrets. Thenceforth my lot was to be cast among strangers, and sorely did I miss the comforting, sympathizing monitor who for some years had been teaching me more than I could teach him; but all my prayers had been answered, all my labours crowned; and with other duties before me I was enabled to look at the past, to thank God, and to take courage.

LETTER XVI.

A REMOVAL.

Circumstances led me to decide on removing nearer the metropolis; and with reluctance I bade adieu to Sandhurst, where I had resided five years. Jack was buried under the east window of the chapel of ease at Bagshot, there to rest till roused by the Lord's descending shout, the voice of the archangel, and the trump of God. I am very certain he will rise to glory and immortality. It was a severe trial to part with my school, to dispose of the endeared relics that had furnished a home blessed by my brother's presence, to bid farewell to many kind friends, and cast myself into the great wilderness of London. The feeling that oppressed me was a conviction that I should there find nothing to do; but I prayed to be made useful, and none ever asked work of a heavenly Master in vain. The dreadful famine in the west of Ireland had called forth a stream of English liberality, and collections were made everywhere for relief of the suffering Irish: one was announced at Long Acre Chapel; but before the day arrived the committee put forth a statement that they had abundant funds and required no more. I was then residing in Bloomsbury, daily witnessing the wretchedness of St. Giles's; and on learning this I wrote to Mr. Howels, begging him to say a word to his congregation on behalf of those Irish who were starving at their doors, whose miserable destitution I laid before him as well as I could. He returned me no answer; but on the Sunday morning read my letter from the pulpit, asked his flock to contribute, and collected upwards of fifty pounds, which he gave to me.

Knowing the character of the people so well, and longing to make the relief of their bodily wants subservient to a higher purpose, I resolved to visit in person every case recommended to my notice. Many of my friends stood aghast at the proposal; I should be insulted, murdered, by the Irish savages; no lady could venture there, their language was so dreadful: no delicate person could survive the effects of such a noxious atmosphere. To this I replied that, happily I could not hear their conversation; and as for the unwholesomeness, it could not be worse than Sierra Leone, or other missionary stations where many ladies went. Insult had never yet been my lot among the Irish; and as to murder, it would be martyrdom in such a cause, of which I had little hope. So I turned my fifty pounds into bread, rice, milk, meal, coals, and soup, resolved to give no money, and on the very next day commenced the campaign against starvation and popery in St. Giles's.

For four months I persevered in the work, devoting from four to six hours every day to it; and though I never in the smallest degree concealed or compromised the truth, or failed to place in the strongest light its contrast with the falsehoods taught them, I never experienced a disrespectful or unkind look from one among the hundreds, the thousands who knew me as the enemy of their religion, but the loving friend of their country and of their souls. Often, when I went to visit and relieve some poor dying creature in a cellar or garret, where a dozen wholly unconnected with the sufferer were lodged in the same apartment, have I gathered them all about me by speaking of Ireland with the affection I really feel for it, and then shown them from the Scriptures, in English, or by means of an Irish reader sometimes accompanying me, the only way of salvation, pointing out how very different was that by which they vainly sought it. My plan was to discover such as were too ill to go to the Dispensary for relief, or to select the most distressed objects whom I met there, and to take the bread of life along with the bread that perisheth, into their wretched abodes. I was most ably and zealously helped by that benevolent physician who had always been foremost in every good and compassionate work for the Irish poor: and to whose indefatigable zeal it is chiefly owing that at this day the poor lambs of that distressed flock are still gathered and taught in the schools which it was Donald's supreme delight to superintend. I cannot pass over in silence the devotion of Dr. Pidduck, through many years, to an office the most laborious, most repulsive, and in many respects the most thankless that a professional man can be engaged in—that of ministering to the diseased and filthy population of the district. But many a soul that he has taught in the knowledge of Him whom to know is life eternal, will be found to rejoice with him in the day when their poor bodies shall arise to meet the Lord.

The schools in George-street, to which I have alluded, are the main blessing of the place; they were established long before the Irish gospel was ever introduced there: and they survive the Irish ministry which, alas! has been withdrawn from the spot where God enabled me to plant it. Those schools are a bud of promise in the desolate wilderness, which may the Lord in his own good time cause to blossom again!

This year was memorable for the great struggle respecting the Reform Bill, a measure rendered ruinous by the fatal act that preceded it, in 1829. It was not passed this year, owing to the steadiness of the peers: but it became too evident that it could not long be resisted by one estate against the other two; and it could not be expected that they who had assisted to open the door to admit the serpent's head would persist in keeping out his body. They had taken the first steps down a rapid descent, and to pause was impossible, unless God gave them such a measure of grace as is rarely accorded to those who have betrayed a trust. He that is unfaithful in little will be so *again* in much; and it was not a small thing to dash down the most sacred bulwarks of our national Protestantism. Tory treachery did the deed; and Tory influence was the first to receive a death-wound by means of schedule A.

Eighteen hundred and thirty-two saw the Reform Bill pass. The first act, almost, of this reformed and papalized Parliament was, in the following year, to lop off ten bishoprics from the

Irish Church, by means of the majority thus obtained. It was a base and cruel proceeding, and it exhibited in glaring colours the value of an oath taken by the Romanists against the interests of their system; for of those who had obtained admission to the British Parliament by solemnly swearing to do nothing prejudicial to the Protestant Church, all save three voted for this deadly blow, which was to be followed up by a series of attacks upon its very existence. The wonder was, that any body wondered at this: I never did. I should have greatly marvelled had it been otherwise; for who could expect the "mother and mistress of all churches" to sit in contented equality, not to say in acknowledged inferiority, beside one on which she is sworn through all her orders to set her foot, and to trample it into the dust.

*   *   *

That our abandonment of the Protestant principle, which we know to be according to God's will, was a rejection of his counsel, and a departing from his fear, many are now constrained to confess, by seeing how strictly retributive is the dispensation under which we are laid. Look around, and what do we behold of the fruit of our own way in forming papal alliance? it is evidently judicial. The rapid increase of Popish chapels, and the open efforts at proselytizing made on every side; the establishment of a powerful and wealthy "Institute," for the avowed purpose of extending Popery; and the announcement of general prayer for the restoration of England to the Pope's fold; the powerful wielding of the public press to the same end, and the ready aid afforded by parties who merge their nominal Protestantism in real, heartfelt hostility to the established form of church government and other national institutions; all this we might have expected; we did expect and predict it too, openly enough, when striving against the overthrow of our defences. But who among us could have foreseen the dispensation by which judgement was to begin at the house of God; or the marked retribution that makes the sin of the church the punishment of the church, literally filling us with our own devices, by transfusing Popery into the very veins of the ecclesiastical body! Unquestionably this is the most deadly symptom of all; and while we own that the Lord must, in the way of permission, have done this "evil" against his offending people, we cannot nationally doubt as to the means employed. The great object once attained, of a restored footing in the legislature and other branches of public power, all was surely prepared, as under the Stuarts it ever was, to seize in every possible way the advantage gained; and as the Church of England has been found the surest fortress of Protestant truth, the introduction of false principles among those to whom is committed the preparation of her young men for the ministry, was of all things most desirable.

* * *

I view this falling away on the part of a great number of our clergy as a direct judgment on us for our unfaithful confederacy with Antichristian Rome. I dread its progress, by the elevation to episcopal authority of men holding the tenets in question, or the perversion of those already possessed of it; and if this be permitted, a schism must ensue: all true Christians, both clergy and people, separating from a church that will cast them out and those edifices that now rise before us—the courts of a pure worship, which we love to tread—will become again temples of idolatry, polluted, hateful and accursed. From such an issue may the Lord in his great mercy spare us! We, who consented not to the purpose and deed of those who brought Popery back to power, and others who have repented before God of what they did in ignorance and unbelief, may hope much for ourselves in this peculiar visitation; but alas! who among us is clear from having exceedingly provoked God to chastise us for our many public and private sins! Had Howels lived to this day, how would the walls of his chapel have rung with the warnings that his lips would never have been weary of uttering, while pointing out the finger of God in this domestic visitation of Popery. But he and Donald, who felt it even as he, were mercifully taken away from the evil to come.

During a sojourn of some years a little to the north of London, I devoted myself more to the pen, and found less opportunity for other usefulness than in Sandhurst and London: yet much encouragement was given to labour among the poor neglected Irish, who may be found in every neighbourhood, and to whom few think of taking the gospel in their native tongue—still fewer of bearing with the desperate opposition that Satan will ever shew to the work. We make the deplorable state, morally and physically, of the Irish poor, an excuse first for not going among them at all, and then for relinquishing the work if we do venture to begin it. In both cases it ought to plead for tenfold readiness and perseverance. I always found it perilous to attack the enemy in this stronghold: not from any opposition encountered from the people themselves; far otherwise: they ever received me gladly, and treated me with respect and grateful affection; but Satan has many ways of assailing those whom he desires to hinder, and sometimes his chain is greatly lengthened, for the trial of faith, and perfecting of humility and patience, where they may be sadly lacking. There are spheres of undeniable duty wherein the Christian may often almost if not altogether take up the apostle's declaration, and say, "No man stood by me." This, to the full extent, has never yet been my experience but I have often found many against me, both without and within, when earnestly bent on dealing a blow at the great Antichrist. It is no good sign when all goes on too smoothly.

In 1834 I was induced to undertake what seemed an arduous and alarming office: that of editing a periodical. I commenced it in much prayer, with no little trembling, and actuated by motives not selfsh. That it was not laid down at the end of the second year was owing to the great blessing just then given to my appeals on behalf of the cruelly oppressed and impoverished Irish clergy through its means: and recommencing, at the beginning of the third year, with an ardent desire to promote more than ever the sacred cause of

Protestantism, I found the Lord prospering the work beyond my best hopes; and by his help I continue it to this day. On the subject of the Irish church, I must make a few remarks, connected with my visit to my country, whence I addressed to you the "Letters from Ireland," already published.

LETTER XVII.

IRELAND.

It was my lot to witness, as I have before told you, the first outbreak of what proved to be an organized warfare against the property of the Irish church. It did not assume this form avowedly while the question of conceding the demands of the Romanists was yet in abeyance; but all the manœuvres of Captain Rock, his enlistments, drillings, nightly sallies, and the whole system as developed during my abode in Kilkenny, were but preparatory to what had long been decided on as the first forward step after gaining what they had long clamoured for—a vantage-ground from which to assail the hated fortress of Protestantism. It was at Knocktopher, within sight indeed of the sweet parsonage of Vicarsfield, that the dreadful slaughter occurred in which thirteen policemen fell, murdered. Dr Hamilton's extensive union of Knocktopher and Kilmagany was first attacked: the latter division of the parish lies of the very border of Tipperary, just where the nightly marauders entered the county Kilkenny. The men who had been first trained to the work as Rockites, now called themselves Hurlers, from a sport in which the Kilkenny men excel, and under this name they declared open war against the Established church. One morning Dr. Hamilton was told that some men desired to speak with him: he immediately went to the hall-door, and saw four or five peasants. The carriage way to that door sweeps through a cluster of evergreens which shade the house in front: but beyond them lies a wide expanse of waste ground. The men requested

Dr. Hamilton to step a little on one side, so that the laurels might no longer intercept his view, and on complying he saw this waste ground covered with men, to the number of two or three thousand, armed with the formidable hooked sticks that they used in hurling, and with shillelaghs loaded with lead, besides concealed firearms, and other dangerous weapons. On seeing this, Dr. Hamilton had the presence of mind to retreat backwards towards the door, and I will say the heroism to shut it by means of the stout spring lock, thus at once guarding his house from the enemy, and leaving himself wholly unarmed and defenceless in their power: he had not even a hat on his head. He had taken care to slam the door with such violence as to startle the inhabitants of the house, and thus to apprize them of danger; and now he stood, calm and dignified, waiting the will of his assailants. Many a sanguinary warning had he received, signed in blood, assuring him that his own should speedily be shed: and now the hour seemed to have arrived when those menaces should be made good.

No violence however was attempted: the foremost men told him that he might see how vain resistance must be against such a multitude, perfectly united, and resolved to yield no longer to the demands of a heretic church. They insisted upon his dismissing his proctor, and refraining in future from demanding tithe from the Romanists of his parish; adding many assurances of their determination to put down the system altogether. After thus warning and threatening him, they departed; and he of course lost no time in making known to the government what had occurred, and requesting a strong body of police for the protection of his house and family.

A party was sent down, who lodged in and about Vicarsfield, and for a time all seemed quiet; but at length the hurlers again appeared, surrounding the house in immense numbers. The officer in command of the police formed his men, and a parley was demanded: when the leaders of the insurgents said they would come to terms, but must have a conversation with the police in the open country some little way off, to which the latter most rashly consented, and proceeded to the spot by the bohreen. This little lane has a fence of loose stone on either side the outer ground, rising nearly to the height of the rude wall, so that the men within it were much lower than in the fields around them. There was barely space for two men to walk abreast, and of course no room for movement or manœuvre. The policemen were allowed to proceed for some distance, and then the ruffians on either side suddenly turned on them, pouring down with dreadful impetuosity into the narrow pass, and murdering them almost without resistance.

The terrible work was soon done, and the butchers dispersed. A wounded policeman, who had almost miraculously escaped with his life, ran to the Vicarage, and bursting into the hall, staggered and fell, covered with blood. The panic was of course dreadful: and as soon as possible Dr. and Mrs. Hamilton, disguised and in a common cart, made their escape to Kilkenny, taking shelter with Lord Ormonde, whence they came to England, for ever exiled from their beloved and lovely home, and in fact stripped of every thing; for to recover tithe in that parish was now impossible. The meek pastor, a wreck in body, but evermore cleaving to his Lord, lingered out some years among us, and then departed to where the wicked cease from troubling, and where the weary are at rest.

Several of the murderers were taken, sworn to, repeatedly arraigned, tried, proved guilty, and set at large; because there was not found a jury who could command nerve enough to lay down their own lives and those of their families by finding a verdict against them, though their guilt admitted not even of a doubt. It seemed pretty well understood by both parties that the Irish church was given over for a prey to the teeth of her enemies, and one heavy blow after another from the hands of those who were sworn to uphold her, confirmed the supposition. Attempts were daily made to ascertain how far the enemy might venture; and when it was found that they might use their own discretion, a general resistance to the payment of tithe ensued, and the clergy, particularly in the

South, were soon reduced to abide in their unroofed houses, the utmost pressure of poverty and actual starvation. Yes, had it not been for the ever-ready aid of England, those faithful, zealous, devoted ministers of the everlasting gospel might have been—would have been—literally *starved to death* with their wives and children. Many were nearly so, when they had sold even the last of their books, and every little article they possessed for personal or domestic use, to purchase a scanty meal of potatoes. It could scarcely have been hoped by the friends, or anticipated by the foes of the Protestant church, that through such extremity the persecuted clergy would be conducted, and again restored to their flocks, purified and made brighter by this searching fire.Yet so it was: God gave quietness, and who could make trouble? God had given commandment to bless, and who could reverse it? I was present at a meeting in Freemason's Hall, in December 1835, when the Archbishop of Canterbury, the Bishop of London, with a large number of clergymen, noblemen and gentlemen, assembled to take into consideration the afflicted state of their brethren in Ireland. There was at the outset a decided deprecation of all political topics and allusions: but the speakers found, not excepting the venerable Primate who had enjoined such abstinence from secular topics, that it was utterly impossible to enter upon the subject before them without adverting to the plain root of the matter. The Bishop of London distinctly attributed it all to a neglect of vindicating the majesty of the laws in Ireland; and that neglect he plainly charged on the real culprits, assigning the true motive—a willingness to extinguish the Protestant church in Ireland. The effect of this meeting was very important: it cheered the spirits of God's dear suffering servants, not so much by the liberal supply of immediate temporal aid, as by the open expression of warm sympathy on the part of their English brethren. I can bear witness, for I know the fact, that the Bishop of London laboured in their cause up to the very letter of that sweet command to do even as in similar circumstances he would that others should do unto him. He sought out information;

he arranged, and made it available in the best possible manner; and he put so much heart along with his superior head into the business, that I am very sure he did far more to rescue that precious church than even he himself has any suspicion of. Our dear brethren needed encouragement, such as could only be derived from the fellowship of those who had too long seemed to look upon their calamities with a cold, distant eye; and their malicious enemies wanted the discouragement on the same ground. Their language was, "Persecute them and take them, for there is none to deliver them." So Satan suggested: but as usual he told a lie.

And now I must name one whose memory is indeed most precious to me—the late, the *last* Archbishop of Tuam. The last through the infamous act of striking off the ten bishoprics, including those archiepiscopal sees that had existed from a date long prior to the introduction of Popery into these isles. Dr. Trench was indeed a prelate on the apostolic model; so lovely a character I have rarely met with. Sweetness and tenderness combined with decision the most marked and uncompromising, distinguished him. He had a pastor's heart indeed; the mind which was in Christ Jesus being in him, to the praise of the glory of that grace whereby he was so enabled to shine in his high station. His heart was in his work, and with his brethren. He loved his country with the most ardent devotion of Christian patriotism. He protested to the last against the wicked Bill of 1829, and predicted what has followed. He bent all his energies to oppose the anti-scriptural plan of national education in Ireland, which was one of the series of heavy blows aimed at Protestantism, and one of the hardest. He laboured indefatigably to spread the gospel in Irish among the native race; and from its first opening to its lamented close, my Irish church in St. Giles' was the object of his tenderest concern. His life was shortened by grief for the desolation of the Lord's vineyard in his native land; and by the shameless abandonment even of the poor guards still left against Popish assumption, which permitted the turbulent John M'Hale to parade his antichristian and illegal exhibitions at the very gate of his palace, while the gaudy mass-house lifted its head above his modest, venerable cathedral. That beloved Archbishop is now with Christ; and most blessed is his memory in the church—most dear, and most precious to me. May the Lord grant us many like-minded with him, to stand fast in this evil day of rebuke and blasphemy!

How melancholy is the contrast presented when we turn to another Irishman, who has the name of his country ever glowing on his lip, and her best life-blood reeking on his hands! It is not possible to compute the amount of life lost by assassination alone, through the turbulent doctrines and doings that have "agitated" poor Ireland for the past twenty years, through the perseverance of one individual in seeking the accomplishment of his darling object. What that is, he best knows: what he has sacrificed to attain it, he will know in the day of judgment. What measure of success has crowned his efforts we cannot tell, unless we might venture to determine the precise nature of what he aims at. If it be to benefit his country, he has injured her more than ever any one individual had power to do in the course of a long life. If to replenish his own hoards, and to earn a conspicuous notoriety, he has accomplished it, and it only remains to render up to God an account of the blood shed to secure what cannot avail him in the day of wrath. Unquestionably the Lord has used that man to work out His own high purposes in a wonderful manner. We find him always moving so much like a puppet, that an unseen hand must surely be at the wires; whether an intermediate one, between him and the Almighty, cannot be known. Probably the master-spring lies in the Propaganda at Rome; but we well know, that even so the spring is wholly under His guidance, who worketh all things after the counsel of his own will. We may shudder when we look on this great apostle of all evil, rending the wounds of his poor lacerated country, and dashing from her the soothing draught of peace; but we cannot fear either him or his machinations, seeing how surely God has set him his bounds, which he cannot pass. I never saw this man until the day when an indignant burst of right

English feeling, not to be restrained by the presence of the beloved Prince Consort, prevented his voice from being heard among the honest advocates for African improvement. I saw him then, and never did I look upon a human being with feelings of such mingled horror, compassion, and disgust. Interested as I was in the abolition of Negro slavery, and working with heart and hand for its accomplishment, until it pleased God to crown our efforts with success, still from the moment I heard that Daniel O'Connell had been permitted to stand forth at an anti-slavery meeting, and enrolled with acclamation as a helper in the work, I wholly withdrew from all connexion with the society, and laboured alone, uncontaminated by so degrading an alliance. To estimate him aright, we must explore his bleeding country; we must number up the slain, including those who have paid on the gibbet the forfeiture of lives stained with murder; and we must follow the souls of those victims into an eternity of unutterable woe and endless despair. It is an awful thing for man to possess influence over his fellows: no talent is so rich, none so liable to abuse, and surely none of which the Lord will more rigidly inquire how it has been applied.

It was in the year 1837 that I had the opportunity of judging how far the events subsequent to the passing of that "healing measure" in 1829 had justified the prognostications of its advocates in its reference to Ireland. According to their predictions, I should have found the Established Church flourishing in the warmth of that brotherly love so freely promised by the grateful recipients of the long-sought boon, and doubly secure under the protection of their sworn amity. I should have found the Romish population peaceable, contented, every way improved; dwelling in the sweetest harmony with their Protestant neighbours, and encouraged in all loyalty by a priesthood now become the faithful liegemen of the British crown. Happily I was not disappointed, for I never expected aught but the strongest contrast to this picture, and such I found: Popery rampant, insolent, overbearing, and evidently calculating on soon possessing the land in undisturbed security: Protestantism depressed, discouraged, menaced, and barely enjoying an uncertain toleration, on the one hand from government, on the other from the mass of the Romish populace: the children of the poor removed from those scriptural schools which were rising up on all sides during my former sojourn, and placed under the power of the enemy, backed by full government patronage. I fell in with an army, marched at great expense to the north, which alone was loyal and peaceable, to restrain the exhibition of Protestant principles and devoted attachment to the house of Brunswick; while no movement that I could discover was ever made, of military or constabulary, to intimidate the hosts of Ribbonmen who were known to assemble for preparations, the object of which was a general massacre of all but their own class. Notwithstanding, I also found the persecuted church occupying a higher position, and shining with clearer lustre than ever before: indicating not the approaching success of Antichrist, but the preparedness of God's people to withstand in the evil day, and having done all, to stand. Of course I do not mean in mortal combat; but I do believe the cause of Christ will never be lost, even for a day, in Ireland; and whatever temporary advantage may be gained by his enemies, I believe it will be followed by the triumphing of truth in a very marked manner. The circulation of God's word has been silently going on, and its effects will show themselves in the hour of need. While the oppressed clergy maintained their posts in the face of even a dreadful death to themselves and their little ones, the work proceeded among the people; and there are tens of thousands among those now most confidently calculated on as the passive slaves of Rome, who, in the moment when their services are called for against the people of God, will openly fling off the fetter which has been privately unlocked, and show themselves on the Lord's side. None can estimate the value of the stand made by those ministers, in its bearing on the Christianizing of the country. Had they flinched and failed, the work was at an end. God gave them grace to endure; and they will yet see the glorious event of their patience and faith.